PRAISE FOR
A RICHER RETIREMENT

"Bill Bengen has delivered a tour de force of retirement planning. Although written for retail clients, financial advisors and other professionals will benefit from his analysis of the most difficult problem facing retirement planners: how to make one's "nest egg" last a lifetime. Bengen has quantified the elements and risks underlying how much retirees can spend over a 30-year (or sometimes longer) retirement horizon."

> —**Robert Huebscher**, Founder of Advisor Perspectives and,
> former Vice Chairman, VettaFi and the Toronto Stock Exchange

"*A Richer Retirement* is the most complete, detailed, and readable exposition of retirement spending I have seen. If Bill's marvelous book doesn't cover it, it's not worth worrying about!"

> — **William J. Bernstein**, bestselling author of *The Investor's
> Manifesto: Preparing for Prosperity, Armageddon,
> and Everything in Between*

"No other researcher has explored so deeply how to navigate the complexities of safely taking income out of a retirement portfolio or explained it so clearly that even a novice investor can understand the how and why."

> —**Bob Veres**, Owner, Inside Information

"How much retirees can reasonably spend in retirement is the hardest problem in financial planning, and no one has studied it for as long and with as much rigor as William Bengen. *A Richer Retirement* builds upon his seminal research with the goal of helping retirees maximize their incomes and live their best lives. Chockfull of data and astute observations, it's a tremendous resource for both retirees and their financial advisors."

> —**Christine Benz**, Director of Personal Finance and
> Retirement Planning, Morningstar

"Bill Bengen introduced the field of retirement income planning to financial professionals and academics. This book provides a deeper dive into the factors that influence how much a retiree can safely withdraw from investments to create a lifestyle. How should a retiree deal with investment risk, inflation, the high price of stocks, and longer lifespans? In a style that is both comprehensive and a delight to read, Bill demystifies investing and spending for today's retiree."

—**Michael Finke**, Professor and Expert in Retirement Investing, Income Planning, and Life Satisfaction

"For the past thirty years, William Bengen's sustainable spending research has served as the heart and soul of the "Total Return" retirement income style. *A Richer Retirement* documents what all he has learned and pushes the analysis forward with new techniques for maximizing the spending power of your retirement investments."

—**Wade Pfau, Ph.D., CFA, RICP**, Author of *Retirement Planning Guidebook: Navigating the Important Decisions for Retirement Success*

"Bengen delivers a well-researched, rigorous, and readable book that clearly presents the methodology and assumptions required to develop a safe withdrawal rate while providing valuable insights into the risks of withdrawal strategies in retirement. Importantly he shows how to manage the strategy throughout retirement."

—**Larry Swedroe**, Author of 18 books on investing, including *Enrich Your Future*

"Bill Bengen is one of the preeminent thinkers when it comes to retirement income planning. To call his early research on safe initial withdrawals (SAFEMAX in his speak) and the "4% rule" (or more technically the "4.15% rule") groundbreaking, would be an understatement. In this book, he provides insights into the underlying assumptions of his past studies and how they can affect recommendations (e.g., 4.0% to 4.5% to 4.7%, etc), using a very conversational approach. The book is rich in content and worth a read for anyone interested in learning about how to determine what the "right" spending rate in retirement should be!"

—**David Blanchett**, Portfolio Manager and Head of Retirement Research, PGIM DC Solutions

"As the inventor of the 4% rule, there is no one better than Bill Bengen to walk through what has changed with new research, and what has remained the

same, when it comes to determining a sustainable withdrawal rate in retirement! A must-read for anyone who wants to understand where the 4% rule came from, and how to apply it in today's environment!"
—**Michael Kitces**, Chief Financial Planning Nerd, Kitces.com

"Bill Bengen gave us the first word on Safe Withdrawal Rates. Now he offers a feast, a full exploration of how (and why) we can often take more than his original 4.7 percent."
—**Scott Burns**, Columnist and Creator, Couch Potato Investing

"Decades after he first developed the 4%-rule that explains how much retirees can safely spend each year without running out of money, William Bengen is back with updated advice. His deep dive into the research behind the not-so-simple rule-of-thumb shows do-it-yourself investors how they can safely spend even more in retirement based on their individual circumstances."
—**Mary Beth Franklin**, CFP®, President, RetirePro LLC

"With his new book, Bill Bengen, aka "Mr. 4%", takes the reader with him down his rabbit hole on a journey to a new SAFEMAX portfolio withdrawal rate of 4.7%. He masterfully takes us there using new data and research that is, at the same time, consumer facing and financial advisor friendly. His eight elements of a personal retirement withdrawal plan are wonders of the modern financial planning landscape. Bravo "Mr. 4.7%"!"
—**Bill Yount, MD**, Creator and Cohost, Catching Up to FI

"William Bengen pioneered the 4% rule, and now he's taking it to the next level. In this indispensable guide, he refines decades of research to help retirees spend more, worry less, and enjoy a richer retirement. Scientifically sound and highly readable, this book is a game-changer for anyone managing retirement income."
—**Ryan McLean**, Founder, *Investments Illustrated*

"Retirement is filled with uncertainty, and there are no guarantees in the stock market. Bengen's *A Richer Retirement* serves as a practical guide for investors and retirees who want to minimize risk while maximizing their retirement."
—**Donna Skeels Cygan**, CFP®, Author of *The Joy of Financial Security*

"Bill Bengen is the foremost retirement researcher of our time. *A Richer Retirement* provides the tools, knowledge, and—most importantly—the confidence to live the life you deserve."

—**Sam Dogen**, founder of *Financial Samurai* and bestselling author of *Buy This, Not That* and *Millionaire Milestones*

"Starting in 1994, Bill Bengen has managed to frame both the investment and spending guardrails that retirees should reasonably rely on when analyzing how they should structure their lifestyles from an economic standpoint after they stop working."

—**Evan Simonoff**, Editor-in-Chief, *FA Magazine*

A RICHER RETIREMENT

A RICHER RETIREMENT

SUPERCHARGING
THE 4% RULE TO SPEND
MORE AND ENJOY MORE

WILLIAM P. BENGEN

Published by John Wiley & Sons, Inc., Hoboken, New Jersey.
Published simultaneously in Canada.

For general information on our other products and services or for technical support, please contact our Customer Care Department within the United States at (800) 762-2974, outside the United States at (317) 572-3993 or fax (317) 572-4002.

Wiley also publishes its books in a variety of electronic formats. Some content that appears in print may not be available in electronic formats. For more information about Wiley products, visit our web site at www.wiley.com.

Library of Congress Cataloging-in-Publication Data is Available:

ISBN 9781394343171 (cloth)
ISBN 9781394343188 (ePub)
ISBN 9781394343195 (ePDF)

Cover Design: Wiley
Cover Image: © timursalikhov/stock.adobe.com
Author Photo: Courtesy of Christina M. Bengen

SKY10117428_061325

To Barbara, my wife
"How, oh how, did we ever find one another"

CONTENTS

Appendixes

INTRODUCTION

Will I outlive my money? That question haunts many retirees, particularly those who depend on an investment portfolio to provide a significant portion of their retirement income. It's natural to feel a bit fearful, as for the first time in their lives, most retirees face the prospect of living off only accumulated assets, pension plans, annuities, and Social Security, with limited opportunities for augmenting their lifestyle through employment income. This sense of lack of control over one's future can be unsettling.

Having retired for over ten years, I can attest to these feelings. But the question of outliving one's money intrigued me earlier than most. As a fledgling (but not young) financial advisor in the early 1990s, I helped my clients plan for retirement. Understanding what kind of lifestyle could eventually be supported by my clients' growing retirement accounts became essential, as well as how to optimize their investments within those accounts. Above all, I had to determine how much my clients could safely withdraw each year from their retirement accounts for their entire retirement; in other words, how could I help them not run out of money?

Finding answers to those issues was far more challenging than I had ever imagined. Today, I would immediately search the internet for assistance, but in the early 1990s, that was still a crude research tool. Thus, as a newly minted CFP®, I turned confidently to the half-shelf of financial textbooks I had accumulated from my courses. Astonishingly, I found no guidance whatsoever on the topic. Next, I paged through dozens of financial publications. Again, no help.

Finally, I consulted some of the more experienced advisors in my geographic area (San Diego). I was perplexed at the wide range of answers I received: suggestions were made to withdraw anywhere from 3% to 8% of the portfolio value annually. In addition, some advisors felt clients should invest heavily in stocks during retirement to maximize investment returns and, thereby, withdrawals, while others pooh-poohed the use of stocks at all. Too risky, they opined. It is better to have an all-bond portfolio and enjoy the comfort of a guaranteed income. I was utterly perplexed.

In retrospect, I should not have been surprised at the lack of reliable information available. After all, the issue of "sustainable withdrawals" was just emerging as a major concern of the financial planning profession. The youngest members of the Baby Boomers, born in the late 1940s, were still about twenty years from retirement and were just beginning to think seriously about it. In addition, their generation (also mine) was the first required to contemplate the need for an extended period of non-working income during retirement. Earlier generations rarely lived more than ten years in retirement, so they could literally spend without fear of outliving their money. Thus, their financial advisors, if they even used one, were under no pressure to develop solutions to a problem that until recently hadn't existed.

It was clear to me, however, that the problem was now real, and was heading toward me and my clients like a runaway freight train. Having been educated as an engineer, I viewed it as a challenge, an obstacle to overcome, and with nowhere else to turn, I decided to tackle it on my own. I bought a database of historical returns of various investments and inflation, sat down before my computer, fired up my Lotus 1-2-3 spreadsheet (this was 1993, after all!), and began my research.

I published my first paper on the topic in the October 1994 issue of the *Journal of Financial Planning*, which, unintended by me, gave rise to the term "the 4% rule." Over the last 30 years, I've authored numerous papers on sustainable withdrawals, published a book on the topic (2006), spoken at many financial planning conferences and financial podcasts, and been interviewed by reporters from all the major financial media. I am still amazed at how this has all grown. Interest in the topic seems to continue to expand, not diminish.

My purpose in this book is to provide you, my fellow retirees and aspiring retirees, with the tools required to create and manage a plan for generating income from your retirement investment accounts so they will last your entire lifetime. The process I have developed is the product of thousands of hours of study and rigorous field-testing. It emphasizes getting every last bit of "juice" out of your retirement investments without taking unnecessary risks. If you are one of the fortunate few who can live on 1% annual withdrawals, this book is not for you. It is for the person who has labored and saved their whole life and seeks to enjoy life to the fullest in retirement.

This work is more than just an update to my 2006 book, "Conserving Client Portfolios During Retirement." It incorporates all I have learned about the subject over the last 30 years, especially critical discoveries made relatively recently. Fortunately, many excellent researchers have entered the field in recent years, and I've included (with credit due) material from their work, which I believe will be helpful to you.

I wrote my 2006 book for financial advisors, thus its formal-sounding title. I'm retired from financial advising, but over the years, I've received (and continue to receive) many inquiries about my research from non-professionals. Thus, I decided to write this book for the general public. To that end, I've adopted a conversational tone and avoided professional jargon. Where jargon was inescapable, I tried to explain the concept straightforwardly.

I rely heavily on charts to illustrate my ideas, and I hope you find them useful. I intend to guide you through my thought processes and results as if I were discussing a subject of keen interest with a friend. Please join me on this journey in the same spirit. If you're a financial advisor, I expect you will also find a lot of material of interest in these pages.

Let's preview the contents of this book. In Chapter 1, I'll provide some general background about my methodology, including a historical perspective on stock bear markets, inflation, and withdrawal rates. In Chapter 2, I'll introduce the concept of "SAFEMAX" and explain how I determined that withdrawal rates are closely linked to stock market valuations and the inflationary environment.

In Chapter 3, I'll present the eight Elements of a personal retirement withdrawal plan and discuss why the term "rule" is applicable only when numerous assumptions are specified. In Chapters 4 through 11, we'll examine each of these eight Elements in detail and how modifying them affects your personal withdrawal rate.

In Chapter 12, we'll "put it all together" and create some sample plans, including introducing the "current withdrawal template," a powerful management tool. We'll also test these plans under adverse conditions, identify potential problems, and explore modifying the plans to resolve those issues successfully.

In Chapter 13, we'll study some important issues that don't fit neatly into the preceding chapters. Finally, in Chapter 14, we'll review the essential lessons of our journey together and send you off to create your own successful withdrawal plan!

I hope you find the contents of this book helpful. It's a distillation of a life's work, but it's not likely to be my last word on the topic. There's so much more to learn, and I'm eager to share it with you!

Yours for a fulfilling retirement,

William P. Bengen

January 2025

ACKNOWLEDGMENTS

I am very grateful to my daughter, Jennifer, for her proofreading of this book. All errors remain my responsibility. Thanks also to Jaden Rose Walker and Christina Bengen for providing feedback on some of the contents. I also wish to thank my former financial advising colleagues for their continued encouragement of my research and their ability to maintain an unbored façade when I could not converse about anything else.

CHAPTER 1

THE PROBLEM: OUTLIVING YOUR RETIREMENT SAVINGS

Long-range planning for income from retirement savings is beset with many uncertainties. To begin with, we don't know how long we'll live in retirement. Will it be 20 years? Thirty years? Or will we survive to the ripe old age of 105, as did dear-departed Aunt Matilda?

Furthermore, financial markets are inherently volatile and unpredictable. We don't know what returns to expect from investments such as stocks and bonds in years to come. The future path of inflation is also indeterminate. Will the stock market crash, or will it soar? Will we return to the painful inflation of the 1970s, which mauled the portfolios of retirees, or will the Federal Reserve triumph in its battle to beat it back? As we'll see in later chapters, these are vital considerations for your withdrawal plan.

Long ago, I learned the futility of forecasting any of these factors. I prefer the attitude of one of my favorite authors, Mark Twain, who slyly observed, "Prediction is difficult – particularly when it involves the future." Thus, in the early 1990s, when I tackled the urgent need to guide my clients on retirement withdrawals, I decided to turn toward the past for answers.

1.1 PORTFOLIO LONGEVITY, BEAR MARKETS, AND INFLATION

My research relies heavily on charts to illustrate my findings. You'll find this book loaded to the brim with charts! An updated version of the first chart I ever produced, in 1993, appears in Figure 1.1.

This chart presents, for each of hundreds of historical retirees, the length of time their portfolio lasted (its "longevity"), assuming an initial withdrawal rate of 6%. The 6% rate was chosen arbitrarily. At the time, I had no idea what constituted a reasonable withdrawal rate.

Some clarifications are needed before we engage in observations about this chart.

First, this chart contains data for clients who retired on the first day of each quarter beginning 1 January 1926, and ending 1 January 2013, a total of 349 individuals.

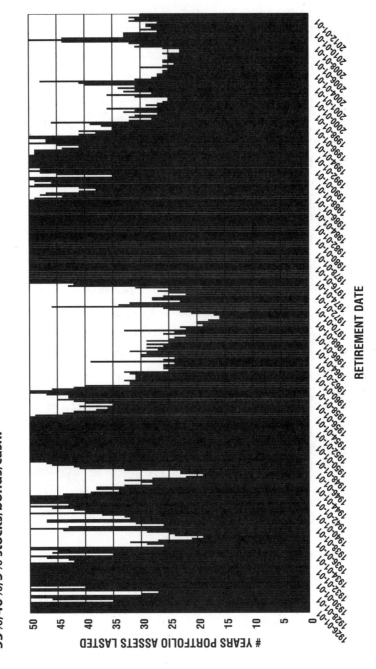

Figure 1.1 Number of years portfolio lasted @ 6% initial withdrawal rate. Tax-advantaged account, cost-of-living adjustment (COLA) scheme, seven asset classes, capped at 50 years, fixed 55%/40%/5% stocks/bonds/cash.

The findings in this book are based on actual data through 31 December 2022. Analysis of retiree portfolios with less than 10 years of actual data can produce unreliable results, so for this chart I excluded individuals who retired after 1 January 2013.

Second, I capped the "longevity" of each portfolio at a maximum of 50 years. There are, of course, a few exceptionally long-lived individuals who will be retired for longer, and many of the "Financial Independence, Retire Early (FIRE)" folks (who aspire to retire at age 35 or younger) may exceed this limitation. However, 50 years is long enough for the great majority of retirees.

Third, those who retired on or after 1 January 1974 lack a full 50 years of actual data. For years with missing data (beginning 1 January 2023), I have inserted long-term averages of investment returns and inflation statistics. This "data gap" is not of great concern, as the longevity of most retirement portfolios is determined in their first decade. This doesn't imply that developments of the last 20 years of retirement are without impact; it's just that earlier events have their effects compounded for longer, and thus those effects are magnified.

Next, we need to specify some of the assumptions made in the preparation of the chart:

1. A "tax-advantaged" account (such as an IRA or Roth IRA).
2. The portfolio "rebalanced" (returned to its original allocation) once annually.
3. Portfolio allocated as follows: 55% in stocks, 40% in bonds, and 5% in cash.
4. Withdrawals made using the "COLA" scheme, which works as follows: The first-year withdrawal equals 6% of the portfolio's starting value. In subsequent years, withdrawals are increased by the prior year's inflation, much as Social Security functions.

Now that we have the preliminaries out of the way, let's take a closer look at Figure 1.1. One is immediately struck by how many portfolios, even at a seemingly high withdrawal rate of 6%, lasted for at least 50 years. More than a third of the retirees fall into this category. Many of these probably lasted considerably longer, but the chart is arbitrarily capped at 50 years. A "6% rule" would have worked for these retirees, and possibly even a higher withdrawal rate!

It's also evident that, in contrast, many retirees ran out of money well short of 50 years, including several who failed to make it to 20 years. These "failed portfolios" seemed to occur in clusters. What's the reason for that?

To answer that question, consider Table 1.1, which lists major bear markets in US Large-Company Stocks since 1926. A bear market is an extended period during which stock prices decline significantly. They are often associated with a recession in the economy. Furthermore, to be considered a bona fide major bear market, investors need to develop a negative psychology, often including a conviction that they "will never buy another stock as long as they live." By these standards, the 33% COVID-related decline in early 2020 does not qualify as a major bear market, as investors did not have enough time to develop FOLM (Fear of Losing Money). In fact, they barely had enough time to swallow their Paxlovid tablets before it was over.

Table 1.1   Characteristics of major bear markets in US large-company stocks (LCS) since 1926

Period	Duration (months)	Total return LCS	Change in inflation	Total return ITGB[*]
September 1929–June 1932	34	−89.2%	−27.8%	+17.6%
March 1937–March 1938	13	−50.0%	+ 0.0%	+3.1%
January 1973–December 1974	24	−48.2%	+22.1%	+10.6%
September 2000–September 2002	25	−49.1%	+4.8%	+9.7%
October 2007–March 2009	17	−56.8%	+1.8%	+15.0%

[*] ITGB = Intermediate-Term US Government Bonds

Perhaps unsurprisingly, most of the dips in Figure 1.1 coincide with the major bear markets listed in Table 1.1. *It's fair to conclude that a major bear market early in retirement tends to significantly reduce portfolio longevity.* Concomitantly, a major bull market early in retirement (such as during the 1980s) can have the felicitous effect of extending a portfolio's life.

There are further lessons to be learned here. Note that the bar corresponding to the October 1947 retiree is notably short (22 years) but is not associated with any major bear market. However, from July 1946 through June 1948, a period of two years, inflation raged at high levels. This clearly indicates that inflation is a critical factor in making retirement portfolios last.

In Table 1.1, the deepest bear market occurred during the Depression, with a loss exceeding 89%. However, according to Figure 1.1, a more severe reduction in portfolio longevity happened a few years prior to the 1973–1974 bear market, which registered a much smaller loss in stock prices (−49.8%). Why didn't the Depression bear market have a more onerous effect on portfolio longevity?

The answer is that the Depression was a time of double-digit *deflation* (declining consumer prices), which reduced withdrawals for several consecutive years. The 1973–1974 bear market occurred during a period of high inflation (rising consumer prices), so that retirement portfolios were subjected to a double whammy of declining portfolio values and rapidly accelerating withdrawals (to better understand this dual effect, see the "balloon analogy" in Section 1.5). There have been other periods as well, when a moderate decline in stocks accompanied by a short burst of high inflation damaged retirement portfolios. In other words, inflation must be considered on a par with stock bear markets as a determinant of the success of a withdrawal plan.

Finally, the last column in Table 1.1 displays the returns earned by US Government Bonds during stock bear markets. The positive returns earned by bonds made them a useful "diversifier" to offset some of the losses in stocks. We shall see further evidence of this effect when we discuss optimum asset allocations for retirement portfolios.

1.2 MY RESEARCH METHODOLOGY

A few words about my research methods seem appropriate. From the beginning, I've used a "historical" or "deterministic" approach to the problem of sustainable withdrawals. That means I use actual historical data on investment returns and inflation to re-create the portfolio experience of individuals who retired in the past. My tools of choice are Excel spreadsheets, which contain millions of cells each. They suit my very "hands-on," visual style of research.

I study a group of retirees who retired on the first day of every quarter, from 1 January 1926. Through 1 January 1993, I have a database of 269 retirees with a full 30 years of data in their portfolios. I call these retirees my "stalwarts."

I study an additional 119 retirees (the last one retired on 1 October 2022) whose portfolios contain only partial data for the last 30 years of their retirement. I filled in the missing data with long-term average returns for each asset class and average consumer price index (CPI) numbers. In that sense, I'm like the geneticist in *Jurassic Park* who inserts frog DNA in his dinosaur genome to bring their creatures to life. Hopefully, my data won't bite me! Not unreasonably, I call these retirees my "combos," as they contain a combination of real and extrapolated data. I use them sparingly and carefully, as it's possible to draw misleading conclusions from them.

Altogether, my 'family' of retirees consists of 388 individuals and grows by four members each year. For each retiree, I construct a 50-year grid on a computer spreadsheet, with one row for each year of retirement. This grid is the source of all the results I present in this book. As an example, consider the individual who retired on 1 July 1961. A portion of their grid is shown in Figure 1.2.

Figure 1.2 Data grid for 1 July 1961 retiree

```
START DATE OF PORTFOLIO:   JUL 1, 1961
START VALUE OF PORTFOLIO:                                                          $100,000  (DRIVEN FROM SCRATCH)
% OF LARGE COMPANY US STOCKS (LCS) IN PORTFOLIO (START):                             11.0%   (DRIVEN FROM SCRATCH)
% OF SMALL COMPANY US STOCKS (SCS) IN PORTFOLIO:                                     11.0%   (DRIVEN FROM SCRATCH)
% OF MID-CAP US STOCKS (MCS) IN PORTFOLIO:                                           11.0%   (DRIVEN FROM SCRATCH)
% OF INTERNATIONAL STOCKS (ITS) IN PORTFOLIO:                                        11.0%   (DRIVEN FROM SCRATCH)
% OF MICRO-CAP US STOCKS (MIC) IN PORTFOLIO:                                         11.0%   (DRIVEN FROM SCRATCH)
% OF US TREASURY BILLS (TB) IN PORTFOLIO:                                             5.0%   (DRIVEN FROM SCRATCH)
% OF INTERMEDIATE-TERM US GOVT BONDS (ITGB) IN PORTFOLIO (FORCED):                   40.0%   (DRIVEN FROM SCRATCH)
REDUCE EQUITIES (& INCREASE BONDS) EACH YEAR BY :                                     0.00%  (DRIVEN FROM SCRATCH)
1ST YEAR WITHDRAWAL:                                                                 $6,000  (DRIVEN FROM SCRATCH)
% OF CAPITAL APPRECIATION DISTRIBUTED & TAXED EACH YEAR:                               70%
TAX RATE ON ORDINARY INCOME:                                                            0%   (DRIVEN FROM SCRATCH)
TAX RATE ON CAPITAL GAINS INCOME:                                                       0%   (DRIVEN FROM SCRATCH)
TOTAL EQUIT:        55.00%          TOTAL FIXED INC:  45.00%      INITIAL WITHDRAWAL RATE:   6.00%
```

MTH	YEAR	#/YR	PORTFOLIO VALUE BOY	LCS TOT ROR	SCS TOT ROR	MCS TOT ROR	ITS TOT ROR	MIC TOT ROR	TB TOT ROR	ITGB TOT ROR	CPI RATE	LCS INC ROR	SCS INC ROR	MCS INC ROR	ITS INC ROR	MIC INC ROR	TB INC ROR	ITGB INC ROR
Jun	1962	1	$100,000	-12.66%	-14.49%	-18.02%	-8.68%	-16.16%	2.35%	3.66%	1.23%	3.19%	0.00%	2.97%	3.88%	0.00%	2.35%	3.70%
Jun	1963	2	$88,247	31.17%	31.12%	28.48%	2.19%	19.07%	2.86%	3.79%	1.33%	4.03%	0.00%	3.77%	4.90%	0.00%	2.86%	3.65%
Jun	1964	3	$93,662	21.52%	18.61%	13.98%	-2.61%	7.94%	3.42%	3.05%	1.33%	3.44%	0.00%	3.13%	4.18%	0.00%	3.42%	3.94%
Jun	1965	4	$94,447	6.15%	15.76%	10.71%	-2.50%	14.31%	3.74%	4.07%	1.95%	3.18%	0.00%	3.14%	3.87%	0.00%	3.74%	4.03%
Jun	1966	5	$94,123	3.98%	35.50%	19.15%	1.71%	36.95%	4.27%	-0.39%	2.55%	3.37%	0.00%	3.48%	4.10%	0.00%	4.27%	4.40%
Jun	1967	6	$97,208	10.73%	34.87%	23.15%	-1.79%	37.36%	4.61%	4.04%	2.68%	3.44%	0.00%	3.30%	4.18%	0.00%	4.61%	4.92%
Jun	1968	7	$102,770	13.40%	47.01%	20.68%	25.68%	64.02%	4.61%	4.72%	4.31%	3.30%	0.00%	3.19%	4.01%	0.00%	4.61%	5.37%
Jun	1969	8	$116,163	1.18%	-0.82%	-3.89%	11.99%	-5.13%	5.72%	1.54%	5.48%	3.16%	0.00%	3.02%	3.84%	0.00%	5.72%	5.76%
Jun	1970	9	$110,568	-22.94%	-44.45%	-29.02%	-7.81%	-44.70%	7.04%	3.59%	6.01%	3.14%	0.00%	2.99%	3.82%	0.00%	7.04%	7.21%
Jun	1971	10	$88,143	41.86%	52.43%	56.26%	21.45%	53.69%	4.99%	11.75%	4.46%	4.27%	0.00%	4.28%	5.19%	0.00%	4.99%	6.60%
Jun	1972	11	$104,259	10.74%	7.67%	9.99%	32.38%	6.52%	4.12%	10.34%	2.88%	3.08%	0.00%	2.96%	3.75%	0.00%	4.12%	5.97%
Jun	1973	12	$107,390	0.17%	-30.76%	-24.75%	26.05%	-39.50%	5.06%	3.81%	5.91%	3.02%	0.00%	2.59%	3.67%	0.00%	5.06%	6.16%
Jun	1974	13	$93,270	-14.48%	-7.64%	-10.73%	-25.35%	-11.76%	8.01%	0.91%	10.95%	3.38%	0.00%	3.52%	4.11%	0.00%	8.01%	6.94%
Jun	1975	14	$78,538	16.08%	39.73%	39.94%	7.54%	38.96%	6.76%	11.30%	9.32%	4.31%	0.00%	4.48%	5.23%	0.00%	6.76%	7.80%
Jun	1976	15	$82,763	13.98%	27.29%	21.62%	5.15%	25.71%	5.51%	8.97%	5.91%	3.96%	0.00%	3.84%	4.81%	0.00%	5.51%	7.49%
Jun	1977	16	$82,192	0.59%	30.04%	13.44%	9.56%	24.34%	4.88%	10.40%	6.90%	4.18%	0.00%	4.18%	5.09%	0.00%	4.88%	6.80%
Jun	1978	17	$79,965	0.12%	38.80%	11.89%	30.25%	40.57%	5.99%	0.88%	7.42%	4.84%	0.00%	4.79%	5.88%	0.00%	5.99%	7.11%
Jun	1979	18	$77,273	13.66%	28.56%	19.41%	17.29%	20.58%	8.97%	8.43%	10.66%	5.61%	0.00%	5.34%	6.81%	0.00%	8.97%	8.47%
Jun	1980	19	$73,641	17.31%	11.74%	19.68%	18.66%	15.27%	11.29%	7.73%	14.58%	5.81%	0.00%	5.57%	7.05%	0.00%	11.29%	9.49%
Jun	1981	20	$66,677	20.51%	69.64%	34.96%	9.36%	58.59%	12.73%	-3.50%	9.57%	5.48%	0.00%	5.45%	6.66%	0.00%	12.72%	10.82%
Jun	1982	21	$60,304	-11.45%	-15.17%	-13.86%	-14.73%	-17.33%	13.52%	13.96%	7.11%	5.29%	0.00%	4.94%	6.42%	0.00%	13.52%	13.71%
Jun	1983	22	$41,372	61.18%	97.65%	76.36%	31.27%	103.19%	8.54%	26.72%	2.58%	6.33%	0.00%	6.21%	7.68%	0.00%	8.54%	12.02%
Jun	1984	23	$33,191	-4.53%	-11.40%	-12.54%	11.41%	-19.59%	9.37%	2.81%	4.23%	4.44%	0.00%	4.04%	5.40%	0.00%	9.37%	11.09%
Jun	1985	24	$12,862	30.81%	15.09%	31.57%	23.74%	14.35%	9.02%	27.42%	3.72%	4.96%	0.00%	4.70%	6.02%	0.00%	9.02%	11.98%
Jun	1986	25	$0	35.81%	30.46%	34.21%	89.90%	32.01%	7.12%	17.86%	1.77%	4.20%	0.00%	3.98%	5.10%	0.00%	7.12%	8.96%
Jun	1987	26	$0	25.29%	7.92%	17.83%	58.73%	2.96%	5.53%	5.74%	3.72%	3.51%	0.00%	3.27%	4.27%	0.00%	5.53%	7.18%
Jun	1988	27	$0	-5.90%	-4.85%	0.06%	4.32%	-10.25%	5.50%	7.77%	3.95%	3.05%	0.00%	2.94%	3.71%	0.00%	5.50%	8.09%
Jun	1989	28	$0	20.62%	10.79%	16.86%	9.78%	9.11%	7.79%	10.79%	5.16%	3.87%	0.00%	3.59%	4.71%	0.00%	7.79%	8.50%
Jun	1990	29	$0	16.50%	-1.17%	6.19%	3.53%	-4.98%	8.12%	6.36%	4.67%	3.72%	0.00%	3.37%	4.53%	0.00%	8.12%	7.94%
Jun	1991	30	$0	7.39%	-2.11%	10.12%	-11.23%	-0.55%	6.84%	10.78%	4.69%	3.42%	0.00%	3.18%	4.16%	0.00%	6.84%	8.03%
Jun	1992	31	$0	13.43%	17.41%	15.56%	-0.31%	18.91%	4.57%	14.40%	3.09%	3.34%	0.00%	3.27%	4.07%	0.00%	4.57%	7.21%
Jun	1993	32	$0	13.65%	27.35%	26.49%	20.70%	27.87%	3.03%	13.70%	2.98%	3.10%	0.00%	3.10%	3.78%	0.00%	3.03%	5.94%
Jun	1994	33	$0	1.37%	12.61%	1.32%	17.30%	7.14%	3.13%	-2.79%	2.50%	2.81%	0.00%	2.72%	3.42%	0.00%	3.13%	5.35%
Jun	1995	34	$0	26.09%	25.45%	22.40%	1.95%	22.15%	5.05%	11.09%	3.04%	3.05%	0.00%	2.87%	3.71%	0.00%	5.05%	6.95%
Jun	1996	35	$0	25.99%	30.34%	23.43%	13.62%	30.13%	5.34%	2.82%	2.75%	2.64%	0.00%	2.53%	3.22%	0.00%	5.34%	5.77%
Jun	1997	36	$0	34.66%	9.97%	18.54%	13.16%	10.90%	5.28%	6.87%	2.30%	2.24%	0.00%	2.00%	2.72%	0.00%	5.28%	6.34%
Jun	1998	37	$0	30.21%	18.06%	21.10%	6.38%	18.96%	5.14%	9.85%	1.89%	1.86%	0.00%	1.78%	2.76%	0.00%	5.14%	5.88%
Jun	1999	38	$0	22.74%	-2.28%	9.38%	8.19%	-1.66%	4.64%	3.85%	1.94%	1.45%	0.00%	1.23%	1.76%	0.00%	4.64%	5.10%
Jun	2000	39	$0	7.25%	29.81%	12.80%	17.44%	23.52%	5.13%	4.77%	3.67%	1.23%	0.00%	1.23%	1.50%	0.00%	5.13%	6.06%
Jun	2001	40	$0	-14.82%	6.87%	-5.09%	-23.51%	3.68%	5.53%	10.35%	3.31%	1.07%	0.00%	1.05%	1.31%	0.00%	5.53%	5.07%
Jun	2002	41	$0	-17.98%	2.84%	-10.77%	-9.22%	4.12%	2.28%	9.76%	1.08%	1.31%	0.00%	1.26%	1.60%	0.00%	2.28%	4.57%
Jun	2003	42	$0	0.25%	3.14%	3.36%	-6.06%	15.02%	1.41%	11.93%	2.11%	1.63%	0.00%	1.53%	1.98%	0.00%	1.41%	3.18%
Jun	2004	43	$0	19.10%	40.12%	30.29%	32.85%	43.43%	0.85%	-1.96%	2.27%	1.90%	0.00%	1.93%	2.32%	0.00%	0.85%	3.02%
Jun	2005	44	$0	6.30%	8.00%	13.96%	14.13%	5.91%	1.94%	4.88%	3.25%	1.80%	0.00%	1.74%	2.20%	0.00%	1.94%	3.66%
Jun	2006	45	$0	8.62%	15.48%	12.78%	27.07%	15.74%	4.05%	-1.52%	2.52%	1.93%	0.00%	1.89%	2.36%	0.00%	4.05%	4.23%
Jun	2007	46	$0	20.59%	15.99%	22.93%	27.54%	16.33%	5.06%	5.52%	4.47%	2.04%	0.00%	1.91%	2.49%	0.00%	5.06%	4.68%
Jun	2008	47	$0	-13.11%	-22.63%	-13.27%	-10.16%	-26.15%	3.15%	11.47%	5.02%	1.92%	0.00%	1.76%	2.34%	0.00%	3.15%	3.82%
Jun	2009	48	$0	-26.22%	-23.55%	-26.43%	-30.96%	-12.15%	0.61%	5.51%	-1.42%	1.99%	0.00%	1.84%	2.43%	0.00%	0.61%	2.40%
Jun	2010	49	$0	14.42%	23.47%	26.82%	6.38%	26.88%	0.08%	7.70%	1.03%	2.39%	0.00%	2.28%	2.91%	0.00%	0.08%	2.36%
Jun	2011	50	$0	30.68%	37.27%	42.90%	30.93%	30.52%	0.11%	5.41%	3.55%	2.37%	0.00%	2.37%	2.89%	0.00%	0.11%	1.74%

There are columns for each investment in their portfolio (I currently use seven), in which I enter the rates of total return and dividends earned each year. There's also a column for the inflation rate (CPI) each year. There are dozens more columns (not shown) that compute the dollar returns earned each year by each investment, the dollar withdrawal, the beginning and ending portfolio values, portfolio returns, and other statistics that prove useful in my analysis. Yes, that's a lot of numbers!

Three-hundred-and-eighty-eight retirees is obviously a much more extensive database than when I began working on this project in 1993. However, it's still a relatively small sample of data, given the complex phenomena I'm studying. It's therefore essential to recognize that any results I present in this book are subject to change, owing to the dynamic nature of financial markets. I'll repeat this warning in various places in this book, and I hope you don't get tired of it, but it's too important a message to chance it being overlooked.

My deterministic approach contrasts with the "stochastic" methodology of most other researchers who have entered the field since I did my first research. They develop mathematical models of stock and bond returns and inflation and use computer software to run thousands of simulations. Their outcomes don't represent actual historical performance, but rather portfolio performance that was statistically possible, based on their definition of the relationship between the variables they are considering.

Which approach is best? I confess I'm partial to my own methodology, having used it for 30 years. However, in all honesty, both methods yield approximately the same results. That's not surprising, as we are studying the same "animal"; it would be concerning if our outcomes differed significantly. You should, however, be aware of one shortcoming of both: neither can predict the future. They reflect only past relationships between data, which, as I indicated earlier, may change in the future.

An analysis of how retirement portfolios have performed in the past is no guarantee of future behavior. The word "safe" in my research is merely descriptive, not prescriptive. The so-called "4% Rule" is not an immutable law, like Newton's Laws of Motion. As we shall see, the "safe" withdrawal rate has been higher in the past, and it may be lower in the future. It's very important to recognize that fact; we must remain humble in the face of ever-changing market dynamics. It's never wise to be complacent about one's retirement portfolio, particularly if it represents a significant source of one's income during the "golden years."

Caveat retiree!

Using the power of the spreadsheet, I can test the effects on the withdrawal rate of modifying the many variables I employ: asset allocation, planning horizon, tax rate, terminal portfolio value, etc. As my research progressed, I enhanced my spreadsheets to test more variables, such as portfolio rebalancing intervals and different withdrawal schemes. These ever-expanding efforts have led me to a richer understanding of the complex interplay of the choices available to retirees and their effects on their withdrawal rate.

1.3 GENESIS OF THE "4% RULE"

In my earliest research, I used only two types of investments, or "asset classes" (as they are referred to by advisors): Intermediate-Term US Government Bonds, and US Large-Company Stocks. "US Intermediate-Term US Government Bonds" refers to the bonds of approximately five years maturity issued by the US Treasury to finance the public debt of the United States Government. "US Large-Company Stocks" refers to the publicly issued stocks of large companies listed on US stock exchanges, such as Wal-Mart, Home Depot, IBM, Tesla, etc.

Two assets hardly constitute the kind of well-diversified portfolio constructed by most advisors, but it allowed me to obtain preliminary results
without drowning in complexity. I began to get some answers. It was exhil-
arating. It still is. Okay, so I'm a nerd!

My very first research result, obtained in 1993, determined a maximum "safe" withdrawal rate of 4.15% for all the retirees I had under study
at that time. This result was predicated on a withdrawal of 4.15% of the
starting portfolio value in the first year. In subsequent years, the withdrawal amount increased with inflation, much as Social Security works
(this is the COLA withdrawal scheme, as described earlier). It also assumed
withdrawing from a "tax-advantaged" account (such as an IRA), a zero
portfolio balance at the end of 30 years, a fixed 60% stock/40% bond allocation, and annual portfolio "rebalancing." A few other assumptions also
were made, which we'll discuss in later chapters.

By the term "safe," I meant that 4.15% represented the "worst-case"
scenario for any retiree since 1 January 1926. In this case, that turned
out to be the 1 October 1968 retiree. Every one of the hundreds of other
retirees in my database since 1 January 1926, withdrawing at an initial
rate of 4.15%, would have successfully navigated *more* than 30 years of
retirement.

I hated that "5" in the second decimal place of the withdrawal rate. I
felt that it implied greater precision than my research justified. In subsequent public discussions, I rounded it downward to 4.1% as a conservative measure. The world being what it is (generally antipathetic toward
decimal points and what comes after them), this was soon further abbre-
viated, and thus the "4% rule" was born. I was (and remain) a reluctant
midwife to this terminology, as it scarcely does justice to the breadth and
depth of my research. But "the rule" has its place, as I'll discuss later in
this book.

Some critics of my method have claimed that the substantial data over-
lap between retirees invalidates my approach. For example, the client who

retired on 1 April 1947 shares 199 quarters of data (out of 200 quarters) with the client who retired on 1 July 1947. However, as we shall see, a difference in only a few quarters of retirement date can lead to large differences in withdrawal rates. I believe that observation justifies my approach.

1.4 RECENT RESEARCH

In the early years of my research, I assumed that all withdrawals were made once per year, at the very end of each year. This was a simplifying assumption, although certainly not realistic; most retirees withdraw from their portfolios more frequently, perhaps monthly. This assumption caused me to compute withdrawal rates that were a bit higher than those experienced by real-world retirees.

As the years passed, I sought to convert to quarterly withdrawals to replicate actual retiree behavior more closely. However, despite the excellence of Microsoft Excel, the spreadsheets thus created, with many millions of formula cells, loaded and operated too slowly for my liking. In recent years, I've computed withdrawals in two separate spreadsheets: beginning-of-the-year (BOY) withdrawals and end-of-the-year (EOY) withdrawals. In a later section, we'll discuss why they produce different results. This bifurcation greatly accelerated the operational speed of my spreadsheets. Virtually all the data and charts I present in this book represent an average of the two approaches, which I believe more closely represents the experience of retirees. Bill Gates, if you read this, can you help? Thank you, sir!

I've also gradually added asset classes to my research to more accurately represent a diversified investment portfolio. The first asset class I added to the original two was US Small-Company Stocks, which represent the publicly held stocks of companies listed on US exchanges with a market value of less than $1 billion. Yes, that qualifies as "small" today! Adding Small-Company Stocks boosted the "4% Rule" to the "4.5% Rule."

I've recently added four asset classes: US Micro-Cap Stocks (market value of under $300 million), US Mid-Cap Stocks (market value between Small-Company and Large-Company Stocks), International Stocks, and US Treasury Bills. The latter comprises public debt issued by the US Treasury in maturities of one year or less. It is often considered a proxy for "Cash" because of its high liquidity and extremely low risk.

The addition of these four new asset classes boosted the "4.5% rule" to the "4.7% rule." There are more asset classes that I could add, such as Real Estate Investment Trusts (REITs), Treasury Inflation-Protected Securities (TIPS), Precious Metals, Commodities, Digital Currencies (such as Bitcoin), Alternative Investments, etc. But the small size of the last "bump" in "The Rule" suggests I am approaching the point of diminishing returns. Even the holy grail of investment diversification has limits on the benefits it can deliver.

1.5   THE "BALLOON" ANALOGY

I'd like to introduce a simple metaphor that may make it easier to visualize the conflicting influences on your retirement portfolio. I suggest you imagine your retirement portfolio as a balloon with two opposing orifices. The fully inflated balloon is your portfolio at the start of retirement, swelling with "air": the savings of a lifetime.

The orifice on the left allows capital gains, dividends, and interest from your investments to enter and increase the size of your balloon. Of course, during a bear market, there are capital losses, not gains, and air may escape through this orifice and decrease the size of your balloon.

The right orifice represents your withdrawals, which continually reduce the amount of air in your "balloon." During periods of high inflation, when withdrawals grow rapidly, this orifice can allow a lot of air to escape. As a result, the balloon can shrink rapidly.

Retirees do best (their portfolios survive for the longest time) when the left orifice allows much air into the balloon, and the right orifice emits air sparingly. These circumstances occur during periods of high investment returns (bull markets) and low inflation. Examples would be the early 1950s, or the late 1980s.

Retirees do worst when investment returns are low and inflation runs hot. The outstanding example of these circumstances is the late 1960s and early 1970s.

Most retirees fall somewhere in between, experiencing moderate inflation and respectable investment returns.

In this chapter, we've become aware that the longevity a retiree can expect from their portfolio depends on inflation and investment returns, particularly during the early years of retirement. Portfolios can be exhausted sooner than desired if the amount withdrawn is not in sync with either of those two factors. In the next chapter, we'll explore a key concept: "SAFEMAX": the highest "safe" withdrawal rate for a given set of parameters, including portfolio longevity.

CHAPTER 2

THE SOLUTION: INTRODUCING "SAFEMAX"

2.1 THE "UNIVERSAL SAFEMAX"

In the last chapter, we observed in Figure 1.1 that a 6% withdrawal rate had sustained the portfolios of many historical retirees for 50 years or more, while other retirees saw their portfolios fail in less than 20 years. It seems natural to ask: Is there a withdrawal rate that, historically, sustained the portfolios of all retirees for some acceptable minimum time, such as 30 years?

The term I apply to such a concept is "SAFEMAX," an abbreviation for SAFE MAXimum withdrawal rate. We've already had a preview of the answer via the original "4% rule" and the current "4.7% Rule." Let's examine how the rule is derived.

We'll begin by modifying Figure 1.1. All that's required to answer the above question is to adjust the 6% withdrawal rate downward gradually until the shortest bar in the figure has a height of exactly 30 years. That happens to occur at a withdrawal rate of 4.7%. The "unlucky" individual who is the source of this low withdrawal rate is the 31 October 1968 retiree, who endured multiple bear markets early in retirement, coupled with an extended period of high inflation. The 1 January 1969 retiree is very close behind in their misery. The outcome of our experiment is depicted in Figure 2.1.

The 4.7% withdrawal rate is what I call the "Universal SAFEMAX": the historical maximum "safe" withdrawal rate for *all* retirees, given the specific assumptions made about account type, desired time portfolio longevity (30 years), asset allocation, etc. This forms the basis of the "4.7% rule," which has supplanted the "4% rule" as I added many new asset classes over the years, as described in Chapter 1.

Returning to Figure 2.1, imagine that for any of the other retirees, you adjusted the withdrawal rate downward until the bar height for that retiree also sat at precisely 30 years. I refer to that as the "Individual SAFEMAX," as it applies only to that particular retiree. Each of the hundreds of retirees in the figure possesses their own individual SAFEMAX. If you were to retire this year, you would have an individual SAFEMAX applicable to you, although it might not be known with certainty for many years.

Remember that the "SAFE" in "Universal SAFEMAX" means that the 4.7% withdrawal rate was successful for all past retirees. It is not a guarantee of "safety" for future retirees. Could the "4.7% rule" fail someday? Certainly! We'll discuss that issue at length later in this book.

Before moving on to the next section, I'd like you to note in Figure 2.1 the long, unbroken string of 50-year bars that follow the 1 April 1969 retiree. This indicates many successive retirees for which the individual SAFEMAX was much higher than 4.7%. It was a great time to retire; ironically, it follows closely upon the worst time to retire in one hundred years!

Figure 2.1 Number of years portfolio lasted @ 4.7% Initial Withdrawal Rate. Tax-advantaged account, COLA scheme, seven asset classes, fixed 55%/40%/5% stocks/bonds/cash, capped @ 50 years.

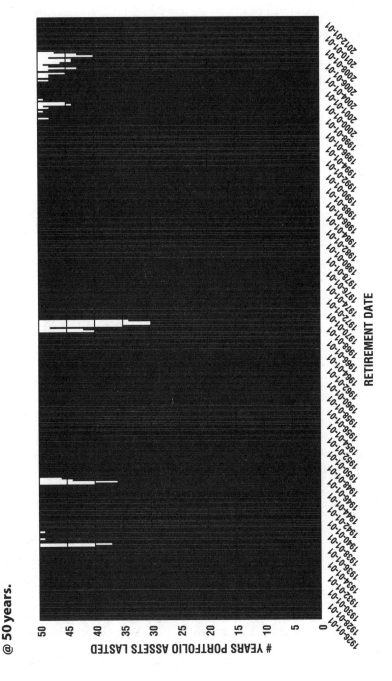

This sudden shift in fortunes was due to the 18-year "secular" (encompassing multiple business cycles) bull market, which began in August 1982, as well as eventual declines in the rate of inflation.

Finally, after the start of the twentieth century, this pattern changed. The two "patches" of shorter bars at the far right of the figure are associated with the major bear markets of 2000–2002 and 2007–2009. Because they stayed well above the height of the 30-year bar, they did not threaten the 4.7% rule. But it certainly appears they made an effort to do so!

2.2   A BRIEF HISTORY OF THE UNIVERSAL SAFEMAX

The Universal SAFEMAX has not always been as low as 4.7%. Figure 2.2 illustrates the evolution of Universal SAFEMAX from 1926 to its most

Figure 2.2   A Brief History of Universal SAFEMAX. Tax-advantaged account, 30 years longevity, seven asset classes, fixed 55%/40%/5% stocks/bonds/cash.

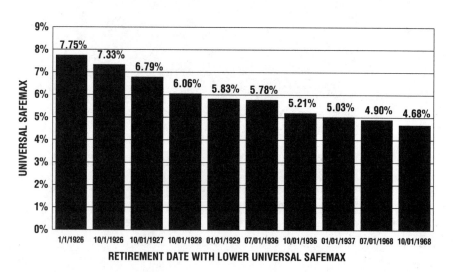

recent incarnation. I apologize to the memory of Stephen Hawking for the title of this figure, which was adapted from his book *A Brief History of Time*, one of my favorite reads.

Note that near the beginning of my data, in 1926 and 1927, the roaring bull market of the 1920s inflated Universal SAFEMAX rates to 7% or higher. However, individuals who retired just a few years later, in January 1929, could not safely manage even a 6% SAFEMAX due to the advent of the Great Depression and the massive bear market that accompanied it.

Universal SAFEMAX fell again, to about 5%, due to the severe 1937 bear market. That level lasted about 30 years until the terrible investment and inflationary environment of the 1960s and early 1970s reduced it to its current 4.7%. There it has stood for the last 56 years, the longest time for which Universal SAFEMAX has remained unchanged.

One might adopt the pessimistic view that after such a long period of stability, Universal SAFEMAX is ripe for a decline. And it might be. However, the investment environment in 1968 and succeeding years was exceedingly hostile for retirees. Despite the coming and going of the dot.com bubble, followed by the residential real estate bubble, we haven't seen comparable conditions since then. Let's hope we don't anytime soon!

2.3 OVER-USE OF THE UNIVERSAL SAFEMAX

When people say they follow the "4% rule" (now the "4.7% rule"), I interpret that to mean they began retirement using the Universal SAFEMAX, or a 4.7% withdrawal rate. However, that may not be their best approach! To illustrate that, consider Figure 2.3.

Figure 2.3 Individual SAFEMAX (1 January 1926–1 January 2013). Tax-advantaged account, 30 years longevity, seven asset classes, 55%/40%/5% stocks/bonds/cash.

This chart depicts the individual SAFEMAX computed for each of 349 retirees (through 1 January 2013), using a 30-year portfolio longevity, a tax-advantaged account, and a portfolio allocated as indicated (plus a few other assumptions). Over time, individual SAFEMAX has oscillated in a wide range, from a high value of 16.2%(!) for the 1 July 1932 retiree to a low value of 4.7% for the 1 October 1968 retiree. The average SAFEMAX for all 349 retirees is approximately 7.1%.

Note that the lowest SAFEMAX of 4.7% applies to only *one* retiree out of 349. All the other retirees had a higher individual SAFEMAX. Therefore, if a retiree indiscriminately used the 4.7% SAFEMAX for their withdrawal plan, they would be sacrificing, on average, about 35% each year in withdrawals, a considerable reduction in lifestyle! The 4.7% rule has applicability, but it should be engaged only when circumstances are appropriate.

On the right side of Figure 2.3, you may observe that SAFEMAX has been trending downward since about 2009. One could argue that the downtrend began as early as 1982, over 40 years ago. This downtrend coincides with an extended ascent to record-high stock market valuations; this is not a coincidence, as there is a strong connection between the two, as we shall see. Except for a few spikes at the end of two major bear markets, SAFEMAX has been consistently below its long-term average of 7.1% for the last several decades. From the viewpoint of retirement income, the last few decades have not been a great time to retire.

Figure 2.4 examines the risks of "under-withdrawing" from another perspective: the accumulated wealth built during retirement. This chart shows the portfolio balance of all retirees at the end of 30 years, assuming their Initial Withdrawal Rate (IWR) matched the Universal SAFEMAX rate of 4.7%. For the 1 October 1968 retiree, of course, the "terminal portfolio value" is zero.

Figure 2.4   Nominal value of portfolio after 30 years (4.7% IWR). Tax-advantaged account, seven asset classes, fixed 55%/40%/5% stocks/bonds/cash, start value = $100,000.

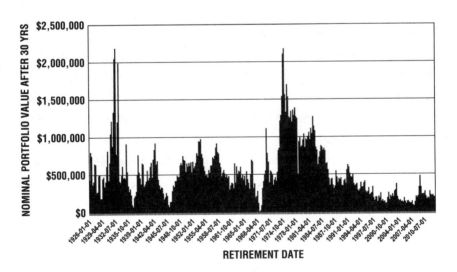

The average portfolio balance for all retirees exceeds $530,000, more than five times its beginning value. At the end of the planning horizon, quite a few retirees accumulated over $1,000,000. Keep in mind that the goal of all these individuals was to have a zero balance at the end of 30 years! *For many of these retirees, the universally "safe" rate was too safe.* They could have enjoyed a far richer retirement lifestyle with justifiably higher withdrawals. In effect, they cheated themselves by defaulting to the Universal SAFEMAX.

2.4 "FEELING LUCKY" METHOD FOR SELECTING A PERSONAL SAFEMAX

It's clear from this discussion that in the past there have been many opportunities for retirees to withdraw at a higher rate than the Universal SAFEMAX of 4.7%. But how do we determine when circumstances are favorable for such a decision? And what withdrawal rate do we choose?

For many years, the only tool available to answer this question was a chart similar to Figure 2.5. It computes the percentage of all retirees in my database whose portfolios were able to navigate 30 years at a variety of withdrawal rates successfully. The Universal SAFEMAX of 4.7% is listed on the far left. By definition, it has a success rate of 100%. Withdrawal rates increase from left to right on the chart. As might be expected, the higher the withdrawal rate, the lower the percentage of client portfolios that were "successful."

As can be seen, the decline in the "success rate" is relatively modest for withdrawal rates up to about 5.25%, after which the drop-off becomes more severe. An Initial Withdrawal Rate of 7.00% is slightly less than a 50–50 proposition. The curve begins to flatten at the far right, but the probability of success is not much above zero for very high withdrawal rates.

Figure 2.5 "Success" rate for various initial withdrawal rates. Tax-advantaged account, 30 years longevity, seven asset classes, fixed 55%/40%/5% stocks/bonds/cash, through 1 January 2013.

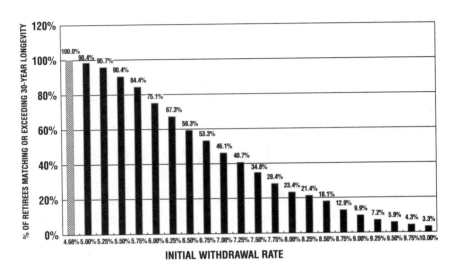

Although this chart has some utility, its most significant shortcoming is that it fails to offer individuals a rational framework for deciding which withdrawal rate to choose for themselves. It begs the question, what "success rate" am I comfortable with? 95%? 90%? 75%? If I choose randomly, will I regret it later in retirement? Will it then be too late to do anything about it?

When I offered clients this chart, I always felt (somewhat guiltily) that I was inviting them to gamble. Perhaps, as per Clint Eastwood in the movie *Dirty Harry*, I was challenging them (disrespectfully) with, "Do I feel lucky? Well, do ya, punk?"

Even more regrettably, it was as if I was sending them off to Vegas to play blackjack, armed with one of those tables instructing them when to stay or take a hit, when to split pairs, when to place an "insurance bet," etc. But losing a hand at blackjack is much less consequential than running out of money during retirement! It was clear that a better guide was needed. But how could that be constructed?

Little did I realize it would take me almost 20 years to devise a satis-fying solution to the dilemma. The final answer would be the outcome of an evolutionary process, partially inspired by other researchers' work and culminating in an "Aha!" moment I experienced early one bright summer morning in 2021.

2.5 SAFEMAX AND STOCK VALUATIONS: THE "KITCES CHART"

Michael Kitces is a renowned financial advisor who offers professional advice to fellow advisors through various media. In a 2008 article, "Is the Safe Withdrawal Rate Sometimes Too Safe?" Kitces published a chart com-paring annual SAFEMAX rates with stock market valuations. A modified and updated version of his chart appears in Figure 2.6.

Figure 2.6   INDIVIDUAL SAFEMAX VS. SHILLER CAPE (1/1/1926–1/1/2013). Tax-advantaged account, 30 years longevity, 7 asset classes, fixed 55%/40%/5% stocks/bonds/cash.

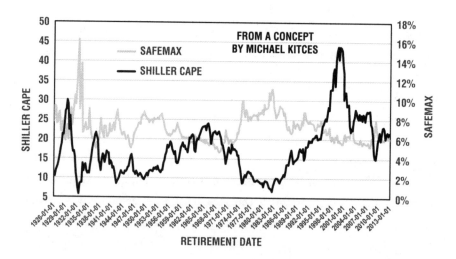

The metric Kitces used to value the stock market (or more specifically, the 500 stocks in the S&P 500 index) is the Shiller Cyclically Adjusted Price-to-Earnings Ratio, or Shiller CAPE. Price-to-earnings ratios (P/E ratios) are a standard tool for valuing an individual stock, or a group of stocks, such as a stock market index. A low P/E corresponds to a low valuation (cheap), and a high P/E corresponds to a high valuation (expensive). Over its long history from 1881 (yes, stocks were around during the Wild West), the Shiller CAPE has fluctuated in value from a low of about five (very cheap) to a high of about 44 (very expensive). The long-term average is about 17.

Single-year P/Es can be misleading, however, as the value of a stock is related to the long-term stream of earnings or dividends the company generates over many years. Company earnings, in the short term, can fluctuate considerably. Thus, the P/E for a single year can dramatically understate or overstate the value of a stock.

Robert Shiller, a Nobel-prize-winning economist and professor at Yale University, attempted to increase the utility of P/E ratios by computing them retroactively as an average over 10 years and adjusting them for inflation. The Shiller CAPE is a broadly used and accepted metric within the financial services industry.

I must confess that I became very excited when I saw Michael's chart. Even a casual examination of Figure 2.6 reveals a strong tendency for SAFEMAX to rise as the Shiller CAPE (measured at the beginning of retirement) falls and vice versa. Peak SAFEMAX seems closely correlated with lows in CAPE, while the lowest SAFEMAX are associated with peaks in CAPE.

This observation begs two questions: Why are SAFEMAX and CAPE inversely related in this manner? And can we use this pattern to select a personal SAFEMAX?

The first question is relatively easy to answer. High CAPE, or high stock market valuations, have historically preceded major stock bear markets. In fact, there has only been one instance of a bear market occurring when stocks were "cheap": during the early 1980s, when the US Federal Reserve Bank, led by Paul Volcker, was fighting rampant inflation by elevating interest rates to unprecedented levels. The result was back-to-back recessions and two modest bear markets. At that time, the Shiller CAPE was in single digits, very low levels historically. Fortunately for retirees of that time, the two bear markets did not cause their SAFEMAX to suffer much, owing to the massive bull market that began in August 1982 and lasted for almost 20 years.

One can think of a bear market as a mechanism by which markets adjust their valuations downward to (and sometimes below!) average historical levels. This process is called "mean reversion," which is a fancy way of saying that what goes up too far must come down and vice versa. As we know from our earlier discussion, a major stock bear market early in retirement tends to reduce SAFEMAX. So, the connection between CAPE and SAFEMAX is direct and meaningful.

The answer to the second question requires some study and is a bit disappointing. Consider Table 2.1, which compares three sets of individuals who retired on two different dates. Each set had approximately the same Shiller CAPE at the start of retirement, but their personal SAFEMAX differed by up to 55%!

Table 2.1 SAFEMAX vs. SHILLER CAPE for selected retirees. (Tax-advantaged accounts, 30 years longevity, 55%/40%/5% stocks/ bonds/cash)

Retirement Date	Shiller CAPE	SAFEMAX	% Difference Low to High SAFEMAX
1 January 1932	9.31	11.30%	
1 April 1984	9.31	9.02%	+25%
1 July 1931	15.52	10.51%	
1 October 1987	15.53	6.78%	+55%
1 April 1967	21.69	5.40%	
1 April 1995	21.64	7.80%	+44%

Admittedly, this is an improvement over the approach taken in Figure 2.5, as the determining factor is an objective metric, the Shiller CAPE at the date of retirement, rather than a pure guess at a "success rate." However, the range of associated SAFEMAX values for a given CAPE is too great to be truly useful. The Kitces chart is a brilliant insight and a big step forward, but something additional was required to better "predict" SAFEMAX for the individual retiree. The search for the Holy Grail continued.

2.6 INFLATION AND SAFEMAX

For years after I published my initial research, I struggled to find a quantifiable link between inflation and SAFEMAX. Qualitatively, the connection was well-established. For example, we know that the Universal SAFEMAX of 4.7% for the 31 October 1968 retiree arose from multiple large bear markets from 1969 through 1974. However, the effects of these bear markets on retirement portfolios was greatly exacerbated by a decade of high inflation, which forced rapid increases in withdrawals.

Conversely, we also know that although the 1929–1932 bear market caused stock prices to plummet by almost 90% (much worse than the 1969–1974 bear markets), the effects of that decline on SAFEMAX for retirees of that era was greatly lessened by the deflationary backdrop of the period. As we saw in Figure 2.2, the individual who retired into the teeth of the Great Depression bear market still managed to enjoy a 5.8% SAFEMAX. These two examples illustrate the potent influence inflation can exert on SAFEMAX, especially if a withdrawal method that adjusts for inflation is used.

Finally, in the summer of 2021, I had an "aha" moment. I decided to test an approach that treated inflation as the dominant factor and stock market valuations as a secondary factor, utterly contrary to my prior efforts. This decision turned out to be the key to unwinding the dilemma.

My first step was to create six arbitrary "inflation regimes." Each inflation regime represented the average inflation rate during the first five years of retirement:

High deflation	Below −5.0%
Moderate deflation	−5.0% to −2.5%
Low deflation	−2.5% to 0.0%
Low inflation	0.0% to +2.5%
Moderate inflation	+2.5% to 5.0%
High inflation	Above 5.0%

Why six regimes? Why not eight? Why not four? To be honest, I don't know. This idea came to me in a flash, and I have not been able to improve upon it through further attempted refinement. It's apparently a near-optimum number of regimes related to the size and variability of my database.

I then grouped my retirees within their respective inflation regimes. Within each regime, I sorted retirees by their starting Shiller CAPE, from low to high. A plot of Shiller CAPE against individual SAFEMAX (within inflation regimes) for all "stalwart" retirees (those with 30 years of historical data) is shown in Figure 2.7. Given the mild inflationary bias of central banks worldwide, I have omitted the three deflationary regimes, as they contain few data points and probably won't be of much use. In other words, we won't likely see anything like the deflationary world of the 1930s in our lifetime!

Figure 2.7   Individual SAFEMAX vs. SHILLER CAPE (sorted within inflation regime). Tax-advantaged account, 30 years longevity, seven asset classes, fixed 55%/40%/5% stocks/bonds/cash.

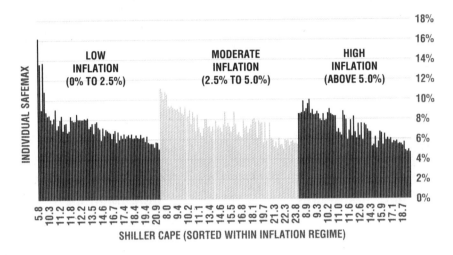

As you can see, within each inflation regime, SAFEMAX generally declines from left to right, with increasing Shiller CAPE. It's a distinct pattern, although not a smooth one. That's to be expected. After all, other factors besides Shiller CAPE and early inflation can impact SAFEMAX. For example, our "two-factor" model doesn't include a provision for bond returns, only for stocks, and only for S&P 500 stocks as well. At 40% of the portfolio, bond returns almost certainly influence SAFEMAX. Furthermore, it's possible that developments later in retirement could significantly affect SAFEMAX. Our two factors are evaluated only at the beginning of retirement.

As soon as I saw this chart, I knew I had a possible solution. But how well does our two-factor model (CAPE and CPI) accurately generate past SAFEMAX? Is it an improvement over the Kitces chart? To study this, I expanded the three inflationary regimes (low, moderate, and high inflation) from Figure 2.7 into three separate charts, one for each regime, as shown in Figures 2.8, 2.9, and 2.10.

Figure 2.8   INDIVIDUAL SAFEMAX VS. SHILLER CAPE (LOW INFLATION REGIME)(THRU 1/1/1993). Tax-advantaged account, 30 years longevity, 7 asset classes, fixed 55%/40%/5% stocks/ bonds/cash.

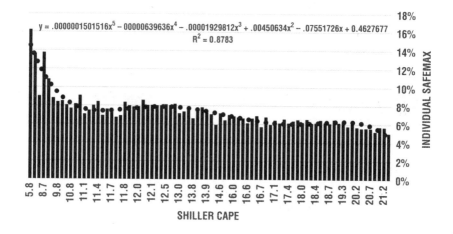

$$y = .0000001501516x^5 - 00000639636x^4 - .00001929812x^3 + .00450634x^2 - .07551726x + 0.4627677$$
$$R^2 = 0.8783$$

Figure 2.9   INDIVIDUAL SAFEMAX VS. SHILLER CAPE (MODERATE INFLATION REGIME)(THRU 1/1/1993). Tax-advantaged account, 30 years longevity, 7 asset classes. fixed 55%/40%/5% stocks/ bonds/cash.

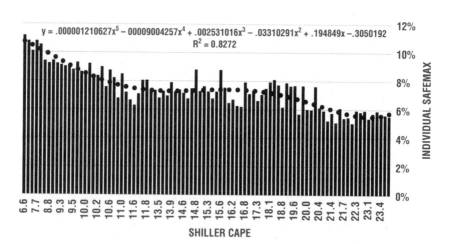

$$y = .000001210627x^5 - 00009004257x^4 + .002531016x^3 - .03310291x^2 + .194849x - .3050192$$
$$R^2 = 0.8272$$

Figure 2.10   INDIVIDUAL SAFEMAX VS. SHILLER CAPE (HIGH INFLATION REGIME)(THRU 1/1/1993). Tax-advantaged account, 30 years longevity, 7 asset classes. fixed 55%/40%/5% stocks/ bonds/cash.

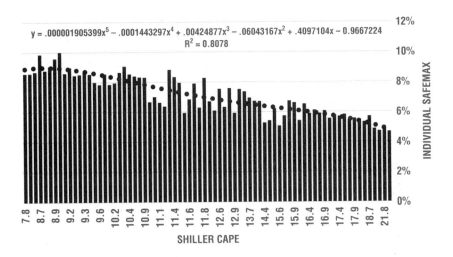

As an example, consider Figure 2.8 for the low inflationary regime. Note that the chart has a curve drawn through the data. This curve was created by special "curve-fitting" software, which seeks to find a curve that best matches our data. The curve is associated with a mathematical formula on the chart.

Let me save you from the trouble of running off to find your high school algebra textbook! In each case, the best-fitting curve was generated by a "polynomial" equation, with five being the highest power of the x variable. Each equation's "y" term is the quantity we are solving for: SAFEMAX. The "x" term in each equation is the value of the Shiller CAPE we supply. As in high school, plug in the x, and out comes the y. Now, you can tell your children (and grandchildren) that you are planning for your retirement using a fifth-order polynomial equation. Won't they be impressed!

Figure 2.8 also contains an "R^2" parameter immediately after the formula. Pronounced "R-squared," this number measures how accurately our curve (and its accompanying formula) fits our data. R^2 ranges between zero (no fit at all) and 1 (a perfect fit).

Note that the R^2 values for all three figures range from 80% to almost 90%. This degree of fit is considered a good agreement between our data and the curve we have chosen to represent them (by comparison, the Kitces chart provides an R^2 of approximately 74%). However, it also implies that between approximately 10% and 20% of the time, SAFEMAX will end up significantly different (higher or lower) than our computed value. These potential discrepancies explain the need to manage your withdrawal plan in retirement, a topic we will explore in great detail in Chapter 12.

You could use Figures 2.8, 2.9, and 2.10 formulas to determine your personal SAFEMAX. However, you didn't pay good money for this book to solve equations! I have done this work for you in Tables 2.2, 2.3, and 2.4, corresponding to the low, moderate, and high inflation regimes. (I'll explain the term "standard configuration" in a little bit. For now, please accept that it refers to the same assumptions which underlie the "4.7% rule.") First, choose a Table whose inflation regime matches your expectation for average inflation during the first five years of your retirement (a crystal ball would be handy for this task). Then, locate the Shiller CAPE at the start of your retirement in the left column, and voilà! Your SAFEMAX appears in the right column. Note that Shiller CAPE data is available on the website https://www.multpl.com/shiller-pe.

Table 2.2 SAFEMAX finder (standard configuration) low inflation regime (CPI between +0.0% and +2.49%)

Beginning Shiller CAPE	Curve-fitted SAFEMAX
6.00 to 6.49	15.37%
6.50 to 6.99	14.11%
7.00 to 7.49	13.01%
7.50 to 7.99	12.03%
8.00 to 8.49	11.17%

Beginning Shiller CAPE	Curve-fitted SAFEMAX
8.50 to 8.99	10.43%
9.00 to 9.49	9.79%
9.50 to 9.99	9.25%
10.00 to 10.49	8.78%
10.50 to 10.99	8.40%
11.00 to 11.49	8.08%
11.50 to 11.99	7.81%
12.00 to 12.49	7.59%
12.50 to 12.99	7.41%
13.00 to 13.49	7.27%
13.50 to 13.99	7.14%
14.00 to 14.49	7.04%
14.50 to 14.99	6.95%
15.00 to 15.49	6.86%
15.50 to 15.99	6.77%
16.00 to 16.49	6.69%
16.50 to 16.99	6.59%
17.00 to 17.49	6.49%
17.50 to 17.99	6.38%
18.00 to 18.49	6.26%
18.50 to 18.99	6.13%
19.00 to 19.49	5.99%
19.50 to 19.99	5.84%
20.00 to 20.49	5.69%
20.50 to 20.99	5.55%
21.00 to 21.49	5.41%
21.50 to 21.99	5.29%

Table 2.3   SAFEMAX finder (standard configuration) moderate inflation regime (CPI between +2.5% and +5.0%)

Beginning Shiller CAPE	Curve-fitted SAFEMAX
6.50 to 6.99	11.04%
7.00 to 7.49	10.77%
7.50 to 7.99	10.40%
8.00 to 8.49	10.00%
8.50 to 8.99	9.53%
9.00 to 9.49	9.09%
9.50 to 9.99	8.68%
10.00 to 10.49	8.30%
10.50 to 10.99	7.97%
11.00 to 11.49	7.70%
11.50 to 11.99	7.49%
12.00 to 12.49	7.34%
12.50 to 12.99	7.24%
13.00 to 13.49	7.19%
13.50 to 13.99	7.18%
14.00 to 14.49	7.20%
14.50 to 14.99	7.24%
15.00 to 15.49	7.29%
15.50 to 15.99	7.34%
16.00 to 16.49	7.38%
16.50 to 16.99	7.40%
17.00 to 17.49	7.39%
17.50 to 17.99	7.35%
18.00 to 18.49	7.26%
18.50 to 18.99	7.12%
19.00 to 19.49	6.95%

Beginning Shiller CAPE	Curve-fitted SAFEMAX
19.50 to 19.99	6.73%
20.00 to 20.49	6.49%
20.50 to 20.99	6.22%
21.00 to 21.49	5.96%
21.50 to 21.99	5.72%
22.00 to 22.49	5.54%
22.50 to 22.99	5.44%
23.00 to 23.49	5.47%
23.50 to 23.99	5.68%

Table 2.4 SAFEMAX finder (Standard configuration) high-inflation regime (CPI 5.0% and above)

Beginning Shiller CAPE	Curve-fitted SAFEMAX (30-year horizon)
8.00 to 8.49	9.02%
8.50 to 8.99	8.95%
9.00 to 9.49	8.75%
9.50 to 9.99	8.48%
10.00 to 10.49	8.16%
10.50 to 10.99	7.83%
11.00 to 11.49	7.51%
11.50 to 11.99	7.22%
12.00 to 12.49	6.96%
12.50 to 12.99	6.73%
13.00 to 13.49	6.55%
13.50 to 13.99	6.40%
14.00 to 14.49	6.29%
14.50 to 14.99	6.20%
15.00 to 15.49	6.13%

(Continued)

Table 2.4   (Continued)

Beginning Shiller CAPE	Curve-fitted SAFEMAX (30-year horizon)
15.50 to 15.99	6.06%
16.00 to 16.49	5.99%
16.50 to 16.99	5.91%
17.00 to 17.49	5.81%
17.50 to 17.99	5.69%
18.00 to 18.49	5.55%
18.50 to 18.99	5.39%
19.00 to 19.49	5.21%
19.50 to 19.99	5.03%
20.00 to 20.49	4.87%
20.50 to 20.99	4.75%
21.00 to 21.49	4.70%
21.50 to 21.99	4.76%

Don't rush to determine your SAFEMAX quite yet, though. First, we have some work to do to customize your personal withdrawal plan. The following eight chapters will discuss the various plan "Elements" for which you must first select values. You may need different tables of SAFEMAX values to match the Elements you choose for your personal withdrawal plan.

2.7   HOW WELL DOES OUR SAFEMAX "FITTED CURVE" AGREE WITH HISTORY?

Let's step back now and take a bird's-eye view of how well our curve-fitting effort for SAFEMAX has succeeded. In Figure 2.11, the gray line (actual

Figure 2.11   ACTUAL VS. "CURVE-FITTED" INDIVIDUAL SAFEMAX. Tax-advantaged account, 30 years longevity, 7 asset classes, fixed 55%/40%/5% stocks/bonds/cash.

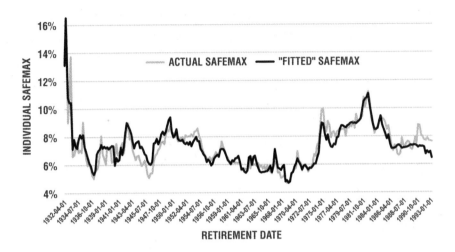

SAFEMAX) is the same one that appeared in Figure 2.6, except all retirees after 1 January 1993 have been omitted, as they do not contain 30 years of actual data. Also omitted are retirees before 1 April 1932, which include all deflationary regimes, for which we did no curve-fitting.

The dark line is the SAFEMAX that was computed from our curve-fitting. Not a bad match, eh? The correlation is much better than when CAPE alone was considered as the sole determinant of SAFEMAX, with about 85% overall.

Clearly, there are some significant divergences on the chart between actual and predicted SAFEMAX. I believe these are all attributable to large and unpredictable shifts in market returns and/or inflation behavior during retirement.

Most notable, perhaps, is the substantial patch of divergences on the far right of the chart, which correspond to retirement dates in the late 1980s and early 1990s. All these portfolios witnessed a massive increase in their Shiller CAPE (stock market valuation) during the 30 years of retirement, some doubling (or more!). This provided a healthy tailwind to investment returns, which supported initial withdrawal rates as high as 8%. In addition, bonds enjoyed a multi-decade bull market, during which their returns were well above average. Retirees of this era would have been justified in increasing their withdrawals from our predicted levels during retirement, a topic we will explore later.

As noted earlier, I've restricted the values of Shiller CAPE in Tables 2.2, 2.3, and 2.4 only to those experienced by my "stalwart" 269-retiree study group, which covers retirement dates of 1 January 1926 through 1 January 1993. Since then, CAPE has soared to much higher levels, in fact the highest in history. However, none of those super-high-CAPE retirees have yet completed 30 years of retirement. As a result, we don't know how their portfolios will ultimately perform; thus, we don't know for sure what their SAFEMAX will eventually be.

For that reason, I'd advise against using the formulas in Figures 2.8, 2.9, and 2.10 to compute SAFEMAX for very high CAPE levels (24 and above). Doing so may yield completely misleading results. We'll discuss how to tackle such high CAPEs in Chapter 13.

This concludes our general examination of the concept of SAFEMAX, the single most important parameter of your personal withdrawal plan. In the next chapter, we'll discuss the eight Elements that set the stage for computing your personal SAFEMAX.

CHAPTER 3

THE EIGHT ELEMENTS OF A PERSONAL RETIREMENT WITHDRAWAL PLAN

In contrast with a simple rule of thumb, such as the "4.7% rule," developing a complete retirement withdrawal plan involves a detailed process, including contemplation of multiple factors. Each retiree is different, and we would expect withdrawal plans to differ considerably from one individual to the next. There is no "one size fits all" in these matters.

In this chapter, we'll conduct a brief overview of the eight Elements I have identified as being critical to the development of a personal withdrawal plan. Each involves personal choices, so they serve to customize your plan to your individual needs. In Chapters 4 through 11, we'll tackle each Element in detail, examining the effect of different choices on SAFEMAX.

Although a decision on all eight is essential to a complete plan, the following sections are presented in approximate order of importance.

3.1 ELEMENT #1: WITHDRAWAL SCHEME

The first step in developing your personal retirement withdrawal plan is to select a "scheme" for withdrawing your money. By the term "scheme," I mean a mathematically defined process for specifying the annual dollar amounts of your withdrawals.

In virtually all my published research, I have employed the "COLA" (formerly labeled "lifestyle") scheme, primarily because of its ease of explanation, as well as its wide range of applicability. It mimics the system used to compute Social Security retirement benefits, as it specifies a first-year dollar withdrawal, then adjusts that withdrawal for inflation each successive year. A great benefit of the COLA withdrawal scheme is that it's intended to maintain a constant inflation-adjusted lifestyle throughout retirement.

One criticism of the COLA scheme is the claim that retirees may spend less later in retirement, so they don't need to maintain the same "lifestyle" later in retirement. This is an excellent issue to consider or discuss with your financial advisor. In my personal affairs, I employ the COLA scheme because it suits my needs well. Even in our mid-70s, my wife and I lead an active lifestyle. We still plan to travel extensively, we love to entertain guests, and our house always seems to need improvements. As long as we remain active, we don't anticipate steep reductions in our living expenses. But your needs may be completely different.

In this book, I'll frequently use the "COLA" withdrawal scheme in my analysis, given its popularity. As I recognize this may not suit others' needs, in Chapter 4, we'll study alternative schemes, such as "fixed annuity," "fixed percentage of portfolio value," "front-loaded," and so on. Note that each retirement withdrawal scheme has its own associated SAFEMAX schedule and that changing it requires a new SAFEMAX computation. New tables to replace Tables 2.2, 2.3, and 2.4 will thus be needed if you choose not to use the COLA scheme. There is no room in this book for all the tables and charts required to serve the great diversity of needs, but over time, I plan to make many available on my website.

3.2 ELEMENT #2: PLANNING HORIZON

Perhaps the most challenging step in developing a withdrawal plan is settling on a "planning horizon," which is closely related to one's life expectancy. I have no profound advice to offer on this topic other than to recommend incorporating a considerable margin of error should you live much longer than you expected. Surely, this is an inconvenient issue to rethink in your late nineties!

Other than that, you might consult your family medical history, use longevity estimation tools on the internet, and discuss the matter with your financial advisor, doctor, astrologer, or palm reader, whoever gives you the most comfort. None of them will know with absolute certainty the correct answer. Ultimately, you must decide.

Thirty years will be this book's default planning horizon, but this can vary tremendously between individuals. In Chapter 5, we'll study the effects on SAFEMAX of a wide spectrum of planning horizons, including those of the "Methuselah retiree."

3.3 ELEMENT #3: TAXABLE VS. NON-TAXABLE PORTFOLIOS

My methodology assumes that the investment account used to fund withdrawals during retirement will pay all the income taxes generated by its investment income: realized gains, dividends, and interest. For a tax-advantaged account, by definition, those taxes are zero. I don't concern myself with the taxation of withdrawals from such accounts, as this money has left the portfolio, and I analyze only what happens to funds when they are still part of the portfolio.

Taxable accounts, of course, generate taxable income on their investments. Since, under my methods, such accounts will pay their own taxes, they will have a lower SAFEMAX than tax-advantaged accounts, as the taxes steadily erode their capital during retirement. The analysis of taxable accounts is made further complex by the various income tax brackets individuals are subject to.

Most of the SAFEMAX charts in this book are prepared for tax-advantaged accounts because of the simplicity of the computations and the prevalent use of such accounts for retirement income. In Chapter 6, I analyze taxable accounts for various average tax brackets and demonstrate the effects of taxation upon SAFEMAX. It would be ideal to have a set of charts for each tax bracket, but in their absence (due to sheer complexity), I present a "quick-and-dirty" approach for adjusting the tax-advantaged SAFEMAX to fit taxable accounts.

It's possible that during retirement, you may withdraw from more than one account, having exhausted the account you began with. To complicate matters further, one may be a taxable account, and one a tax-advantaged account. How do we compute an overall SAFEMAX for such a situation?

An approach to this dilemma might be to withdraw from each account simultaneously, each account assigned its own appropriate SAFEMAX. Alternatively, one could interpolate a "blended" SAFEMAX for use with both accounts in succession. This is probably an acceptable approximation given the many uncertainties in retirement withdrawals. Your financial advisor may have software that can address this problem more elegantly.

3.4   ELEMENT #4: LEAVING A LEGACY TO HEIRS

Implicit in the concept of SAFEMAX is that the portfolio will have a desired minimum value at the end of the planning horizon. As a default, we assume the value is zero, so the portfolio expires at the same moment as its owner. Aside from the fact this is a neat trick to pull off, some individuals wish to leave a legacy to their heirs, in the form of a positive balance in their retirement portfolio at the end of the planning horizon. This issue and its effect on SAFEMAX is discussed in Chapter 7.

3.5   ELEMENT #5: ASSET ALLOCATION

The particular mix of stock and bond investments used in a portfolio can profoundly affect its longevity. In most cases in this book, we assume a well-diversified portfolio of seven different asset classes, allocated in a fixed manner to 55% in stock funds, and 40% in bond funds, and 5% in cash. In Chapter 8, we consider the consequences of departing from this assumption. The results can be quite extraordinary.

3.6 ELEMENT #6: PORTFOLIO REBALANCING FREQUENCY

"Rebalancing" refers to the process by which a portfolio is restored to its original asset allocation by buying and selling its component investments. My analysis, as well as that of others, indicates that periodic rebalancing can be of considerable benefit to the investor.

Retirement portfolios must be actively managed in this regard, as the much higher rate of return of stocks vs. bonds causes stocks to overwhelm a portfolio if they are not periodically sold down to their desired allocation. In Chapter 9, we study the optimum time between "rebalances," with conclusions that may be surprising.

3.7 ELEMENT #7: THE SUPERINVESTOR: STRIVING FOR ABOVE-MARKET RETURNS

The assumed investments in this book are funds (mutual funds and exchange-traded funds) that closely track an index for a specific asset class, such as US Large-Company Stocks, US Small-Company Stocks, etc. In other words, I assume the retiree is content to receive the "market return" for the investments utilized. In Chapter 10, we examine the risks and rewards of attempting to "beat the market."

3.8 ELEMENT #8: WITHDRAWAL TIMING

Most retirees withdraw money from their portfolios periodically during the year, which is the assumption underlying all the analysis in this book. It's worth noting that consistently withdrawing all funds from the portfolio at the beginning of the year will substantially reduce SAFEMAX, while withdrawing all funds from the portfolio at the end of each year will have the opposite effect. There may be legitimate reasons for doing so. We'll explore this in Chapter 11.

3.9 THE "STANDARD CONFIGURATION" FOR THE "4.7% RULE"

In the following eight chapters, we'll take a deep dive into each of the eight Elements, exploring how changes in each Element impact SAFEMAX. It would be helpful to have a default arrangement of the eight Elements that we could refer to with a single expression, the "Standard Configuration." The default values in Table 3.1 are assigned to each of the eight Elements.

Table 3.1 "Standard configuration" of the eight Elements

Element	Option Selected
#1: Withdrawal scheme	COLA
#2: Planning horizon	30 years
#3: Taxable vs. non-taxable portfolios	Tax-advantaged (IRA or Roth IRA)
#4: Leaving a legacy to heirs	None
#5: Asset allocation	Fixed 55% stocks/40% bonds/5% US Treasury Bills (five stock classes equally weighted @11%)
#6: Portfolio rebalancing frequency	1 year
#7: The "Superinvestor"	Not applicable; accept "market" returns
#8: Withdrawal timing	Equally spaced during the year

These "standard values" for the eight Elements are arbitrary but represent the configuration associated with the "4.7% rule." Defining this configuration of the eight Elements as "standard" gives us a convenient conversational tool for future discussions.

CHAPTER 4

ELEMENT #1: WITHDRAWAL SCHEMES

4.1 "COLA" WITHDRAWAL SCHEME

We've already engaged in a detailed discussion of this withdrawal scheme, so spending much time on it here is unnecessary.

As you may recall, the COLA scheme provides a stream of income adjusted annually for inflation. Although I believe that the COLA scheme fits the needs of the great majority of retirees, there are valid reasons why an individual might choose another scheme. In this chapter, we'll consider several alternatives to the COLA withdrawal scheme, which I use most frequently in the presentation of my research. Let's look at some of the other choices.

4.2 "FIXED ANNUITY" WITHDRAWAL SCHEME

Let's imagine that an individual desires to withdraw a fixed dollar amount each year, with no adjustments for inflation or other considerations. As an example of such a scheme, an individual withdraws precisely $5,000 from their portfolio every year. If they begin with a $100,000 portfolio, that equates to a 5% initial withdrawal rate. This concept is akin to a "fixed annuity" (FA), which may be purchased from an insurance company and provides a continual, fixed stream of income for the lifetime of its beneficiary. However, in this case, the retiree assumes the "mortality risk," which means they must guarantee that the payments will not end too soon.

Why would a retiree choose such a scheme? Perhaps their retirement savings are small in comparison with their other sources of income, and they don't want to be bothered with making annual inflation adjustments to their withdrawals. In that case, they would instruct the custodian of their funds to pay them a fixed dollar amount periodically and never change those instructions. Or perhaps they believe an inflation adjustment is unnecessary, as their income needs will diminish as they age. Another possibility is that withdrawals from the account would be dedicated to exclusively paying a fixed periodic liability, such as monthly home mortgage payments.

Figure 4.1 computes SAFEMAX for all (1 January 1926 through 1 January 2013) retirees using a fixed annuity scheme and compares it to the SAFEMAX computed earlier for the COLA scheme. At the outset, we might expect that the annuity scheme would always have a higher SAFEMAX than the COLA scheme, as the inflation-boosted withdrawals from the COLA scheme would more rapidly consume the portfolio.

Figure 4.1   Individual SAFEMAX for "Fixed Annuity" and "COLA" withdrawal schemes (1 January 1926–1 January 2013). Tax-advantaged account, 30 years longevity, seven asset classes, 55%/40%/5% stocks/bonds/cash.

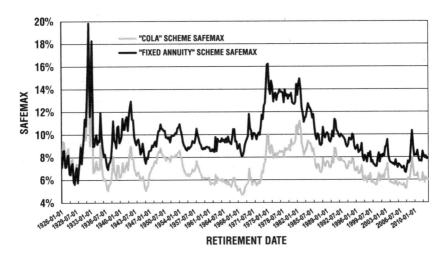

It thus might be surprising to see on the left side of Figure 4.1, corresponding to the period 1926–1930, that the COLA scheme has the higher SAFEMAX! What is going on here? The explanation is that 1926 through 1930 was an era of deflation, meaning COLA-adjusted withdrawals declined yearly. This phenomenon allowed the COLA portfolio to grow more rapidly than the FA portfolio, resulting in a higher SAFEMAX.

After 1930, however, the performance of the FA portfolio conforms, without exception, to our original expectations: it always has had the higher SAFEMAX. The high deflation rates around the time of the Great Depression were unique in the last hundred years, and it seems unlikely we will see their repetition anytime soon. But who knows for sure?

Note that the Universal SAFEMAX (the worst-case scenario) of 5.8% for the FA scheme occurs with the January 1, 1929 retiree. Recall that the Universal SAFEMAX of the COLA scheme, 4.7%, happened with the October 1, 1968 retiree. The difference in dates is explained by the fact that the FA scheme is most negatively impacted by deflation, while the COLA scheme is adversely affected by inflation.

This difference is emphasized by comparing the spacing between the two lines in Figure 4.1. During the first half of the 1960s, SAFEMAX for the FA and COLA schemes were separated by a relatively stable amount, about 3.5%. As inflation picked up in the late 1960s and into the 1970s, the lines began to diverge until, about early 1975, a full 6% separated them. After that, as Federal Reserve Chairman Volcker's efforts to tame inflation gained traction, the lines began to converge until, by the early 1980s, they enjoyed an even narrower separation than before.

Because it specifies a fixed dollar withdrawal, the SAFEMAX of the FA scheme is sensitive only to fluctuations in investment returns (primarily stocks) and not inflation. The relationship between FA SAFEMAX and Shiller CAPE at the beginning of retirement is represented in Figure 4.2 for 349 retirees (through 1 January 2013).

Figure 4.2   INDIVIDUAL FA SAFEMAX VS. SHILLER CAPE.
Tax-advantaged account, 30 years longevity, 7 asset classes. fixed 55%/40%/5% stocks/bonds/cash.

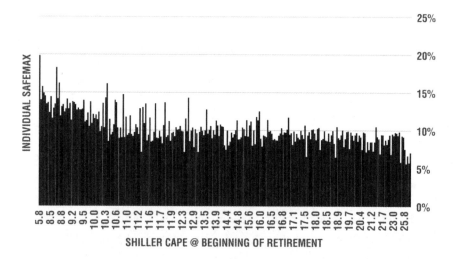

As you may recall, in Chapter 2 I presented three tables for the COLA scheme, which linked SAFEMAX with inflation and Shiller CAPE, a measure of stock market valuation. For the FA scheme, fortunately, since inflation is irrelevant, we need only one table, which appears as Table 4.1. To construct this table, I fit a curve to the graph of Figure 4.2 and derived values for SAFEMAX for different levels of initial CAPE. The degree of fit, about 58%, is not as strong as it was for the COLA scheme.

Table 4.1 SAFEMAX finder (fixed annuity withdrawal scheme). Tax-advantaged account, 30 years longevity, 55%40%/5% stocks/ bonds/cash.

Beginning Shiller CAPE	Curve-fitted SAFEMAX
5.50 to 5.99	18.68%
6.00 to 5.49	17.50%
6.50 to 6.99	16.43%
7.00 to 7.49	15.46%
7.50 to 7.99	14.58%
8.00 to 8.49	13.80%
8.50 to 8.99	13.10%
9.00 to 9.49	12.48%
9.50 to 9.99	11.94%
10.00 to 10.49	11.47%
10.50 to 10.99	11.06%
11.00 to 11.49	10.71%
11.50 to 11.99	10.42%
12.00 to 12.49	10.18%
12.50 to 12.99	9.98%
13.00 to 13.49	9.82%
13.50 to 13.99	9.70%

(Continued)

Table 4.1 (Continued)

Beginning Shiller CAPE	Curve-fitted SAFEMAX
14.00 to 14.49	9.60%
14.50 to 14.99	9.53%
15.00 to 15.49	9.47%
15.50 to 15.99	9.44%
16.00 to 16.49	9.41%
16.50 to 16.99	9.38%
17.00 to 17.49	9.36%
17.50 to 17.99	9.34%
18.00 to 18.49	9.31%
18.50 to 18.99	9.28%
19.00 to 19.49	9.23%
18.50 to 18.99	9.17%
20.00 to 20.49	9.10%
20.50 to 20.99	9.01%
21.00 to 21.49	8.91%
21.50 to 21.99	8.78%
22.00 to 22.49	8.64%
22.50 to 22.99	8.49%
23.00 to 23.49	8.32%
23.50 to 23.99	8.13%
24.00 to 24.49	7.94%
24.50 to 24.99	7.74%
25.00 to 25.49	7.53%
25.50 to 25.99	7.32%
26.00 to 26.49	7.12%
26.50 to 26.99	6.93%

Beginning Shiller CAPE	Curve-fitted SAFEMAX
27.00 to 27.49	6.75%
27.50 to 27.99	6.60%
28.00 to 28.49	6.49%
28.50 to 28.99	6.41%
29.00 to 29.49	6.39%
29.50 to 29.99	6.43%

Across all retirees in this sample, the FA scheme experienced an average SAFEMAX of 9.7%, vs. an average of 7.1% for the COLA scheme. Thus, withdrawals during early retirement under the FA scheme may be much higher than under the COLA scheme. This consideration may interest those who need a higher income stream earlier in retirement and would be satisfied with a lower "real" or inflation-adjusted income stream later in retirement.

Despite generally enjoying a higher SAFEMAX, the FA withdrawal scheme delivers less total income during retirement than the COLA scheme. Figure 4.3 compares the cumulative value of 30 years of withdrawals under the FA and COLA systems for three sample retirees: 1 October 1968 (low SAFEMAX), 1 July 1989 (average SAFEMAX), and 1 January 1975 (high SAFEMAX.) The SAFEMAX used in each case applies to the specific withdrawal system; for each retiree, the FA SAFEMAX was significantly higher than the COLA SAFEMAX.

As you can see, the COLA system's total income was considerably greater in every case. Although the FA system always starts with a higher first-year withdrawal, the COLA system eventually catches and passes it due to the annual inflation adjustments. We may conclude that the FA system should be avoided by a retiree seeking to maximize total income over their retirement.

Figure 4.3 Cumulative withdrawals under COLA and FA systems (three retirees). Tax-advantaged portfolio, 30 years longevity, 55%/40%/5% stocks/bonds/cash.

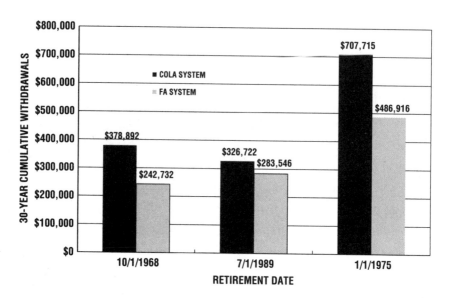

4.3 "FIXED PERCENTAGE" WITHDRAWAL SCHEME

It's a common misconception that the "4.7% rule" means that a retiree withdraws 4.7% of the January 1 portfolio value the first year, 4.7% of the January 1 portfolio value the second year, and so on. Of course, based on our earlier discussion, we know that's not the case, but it *accurately represents* the following withdrawal scheme we will consider, the "Fixed Percentage" scheme (FP).

To some, the FP scheme seems an appealing option. For example, during a stock bear market, the value of one's portfolio will decline, which in return will reduce the following year's withdrawals, thus preserving capital. Once the portfolio recovers, the prior level of withdrawals will eventually be restored. Isn't that a good thing, they ask? Perhaps, on the surface, it is, but boobytraps in the FP scheme need exposure. Let's look at them together.

First, with the aid of Table 4.2, let's examine some of the most significant 12-month portfolio declines beginning with January 1, 1926. Sizeable annual portfolio declines have occurred in the past, some quite recently. They weren't restricted just to the Great Depression.

Table 4.2   Large 12-month portfolio declines since 1 January 1926 (standard 55%/40%/5% stocks/bonds/cash allocation)

Begin Date	12-Month % Change in Portfolio Value
7/1/1932	−33.2%
4/1/1932	−29.9%
4/1/1937	−27.2%
1/1/1931	−25.5%
10/1/1930	−24.5%
1/1/1937	−20.3%
4/1/2008	−19.8%
10/1/1973	−19.6%
10/1/1929	−18.3%
10/1/2021	−16.5%
4/1/1931	−16.3%
1/1/2008	−16.3%
1/1/1930	−15.3%
7/1/1969	−14.6%
7/1/1929	−14.2%
7/1/1930	−13.8%
7/1/2022	−13.7%

For the 12 months following each period in the table, the FP method would reduce dollar withdrawals by the indicated percentage. But most folks can't cut their budgets by 15% to over 30% in a given year; fixed costs would probably render that very difficult. Under what circumstances could an individual tolerate such a sizeable reduction in income from their portfolio? We'll discuss that in greater detail below.

How do we analyze the effectiveness of the FP scheme compared to, let's say, the COLA scheme? We can't use the earlier approach, computing SAFEMAX for a fixed planning horizon, because, in theory, FP portfolios last forever. That's because FP does not withdraw specific dollar amounts from the portfolio each year but rather a percentage of portfolio value. Thus, if there are 62 cents left in the portfolio at the start of the year, and we withdraw 5%, or about three cents, there is still a non-zero balance at the end of the year. The portfolio lives to fight another year. But who will the retiree fight with three cents in their pocket?

Instead, as we did incidentally with the FA scheme, I propose we compute the total dollar withdrawals made from a portfolio over a fixed planning horizon, let's say 30 years, under two different withdrawal schemes. The initial withdrawal rate will be the same for the COLA and FP computations, so we compare apples with apples. We must also select a withdrawal rate no higher than the 30-year SAFEMAX for the COLA portfolio to ensure a minimum of 30 years of withdrawals from the COLA portfolio.

Let's begin our analysis with that most redoubtable of scenarios, our old friend, the "worst-case" 31 October 1968 retiree. Figure 4.4 captures the year-by-year withdrawals from a $100,000 portfolio under the COLA and FP schemes, with an initial withdrawal rate of 4.7% matching the SAFEMAX for the 10/1/1968 retiree.

Over the first 19 years, the COLA scheme generates higher annual withdrawals. In some cases, the COLA withdrawals are almost double

Figure 4.4   12-month withdrawals for "FP" and "COLA" schemes (1 October 1968 retiree) (4.7% IWR). Tax-advantaged account, 30 years longevity, 55%/40%/5% stocks/bonds/cash.

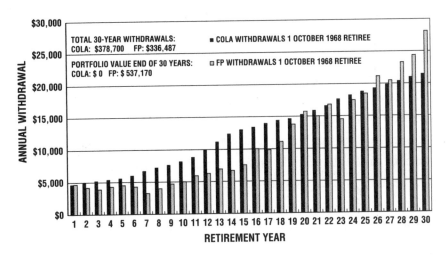

those of the FP scheme! Note also that the COLA withdrawals increase each year (due to inflation adjustments), while in some years, the FP withdrawals decline. (In year #7, FP withdrawals were 28% lower than in year #5. Ouch!) The latter is not surprising, as in years following a decline in portfolio value, FP withdrawals must also decline, by definition.

However, in year #20 and beyond, the FP "catches" up with the COLA scheme and enjoys several years in which it produces higher withdrawal amounts. Despite this amazing surge, if we total all withdrawals over 30 years, the COLA scheme generates $378,700 in withdrawals vs. $336,287 for the FP scheme. That's quite a significant advantage in favor of the COLA scheme.

Notably, at the end of the 30-year horizon, the COLA portfolio is exhausted. In contrast, the FP portfolio still has a mouth-watering balance of $537,000 remaining, more than five times the starting value! This is as it should be, as during all the years when the FP trailed COLA, it was conserving capital, allowing it to generate withdrawals for a more extended period. Of course, a price had to be paid in terms of lower total withdrawals. And that $537,000 balance is worth far less than it appears at first glance, owing to the effects of 30 years of inflation, some of it at annual double-digit rates.

Figures 4.5 and 4.6 show similar data for two other retirees: the 1 January 1975 retiree (high SAFEMAX) and the 1 July 1989 retiree (average SAFEMAX). The pattern for each of these retirees differs from the 1 October 1968 retiree. Withdrawals for both schemes are approximately the same for the first dozen retirement years. After that, the FP scheme badly lags behind the COLA scheme. Overall, the conclusion is the same as before: the COLA scheme is superior for generating a higher income level during the planning horizon.

Figure 4.5   Annual withdrawals for "FP" and "COLA" schemes (1 January 1975 retiree) (10.0% IWR). Tax-advantaged account, 30 years longevity, 55%/40%/5% stocks/bonds/cash.

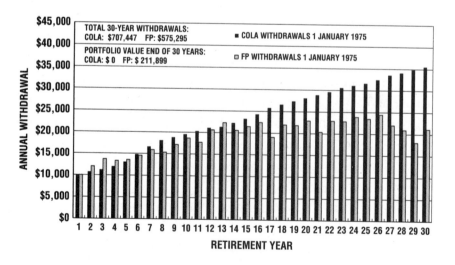

Figure 4.6   12-month withdrawals for "FP" and "COLA" schemes (1 July 1989 retiree) (7.1% IWR). Tax-advantaged account, 30 years longevity, 55%/40%/5% stocks/bonds/cash.

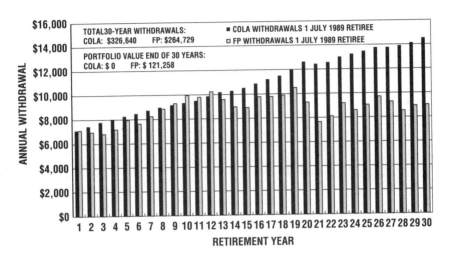

Having examined a few representative portfolios, let's consider a comparison of all retirees from 1 January 1926 to 1 January 2013 (349 retirees in total). Figure 4.7 compares the total value of all withdrawals over 30 years for each retiree under the COLA and the FP scheme. In each case, the individual retiree's initial withdrawal rate (IWR) is set at the COLA SAFEMAX.

In all cases save one, total withdrawals were always greater with the COLA scheme. On average, the COLA scheme produced an impressive 33% higher withdrawals during the 30-year horizon. This confirms the conclusion we reached earlier from our three sample retirees: during the planning horizon, the COLA scheme almost always produced a higher cumulative income than the FP scheme.

The sole exception was the July 1, 1937 retiree, who had 13% higher cumulative withdrawals under the FP scheme. By way of explanation, this individual experienced two years of portfolio losses at the very beginning

Figure 4.7   30-year cumulative withdrawals for "FP" and "COLA" schemes (all retirees). Tax-advantaged account, 30 years longevity, 55%40%5% stocks/bonds/cash, IWR = COLA SAFEMAX

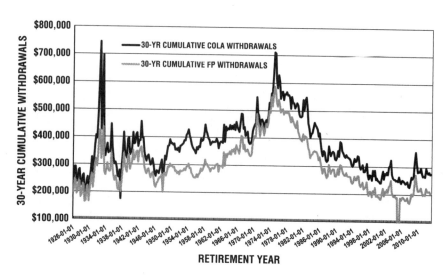

of their retirement (owing mainly to the nasty 1937–1938 stock bear market); 10-year portfolio returns were also relatively weak. In this instance, the FP scheme's property of conserving capital in down markets provided great value.

As an extension of this reasoning, the best relative performance by the FP scheme was for retirees who experienced deep bear markets in stocks early in their retirement. This includes the 1 October 1968 retiree analyzed above and those who retired in 1929–1930, 1942, 1946–1947, 1968–1974, and 1976–1978 (this may also apply to 2007–2008, but it's too early to tell). This effect is evident in Figure 4.7, as the space between the two curves narrows during bear markets and widens during bull markets.

Conversely, the worst relative performance of the FP scheme was for those individuals who retired into powerful bull markets. For example, the July 1, 1932 retiree, who retired just at the end of the huge 1929–1932 bear market, enjoyed 72% higher withdrawals under the COLA system. FDR says thank you very much, COLA scheme!

I thus conclude that the FP scheme is not appropriate for retirees seeking the highest level of income from their portfolio during their planning horizon. However, an individual with another source of income to cover their fixed expenses might select this withdrawal method for a portfolio intended as a "side fund" from which to pay primarily discretionary expenses, which could fluctuate considerably without undue harm. For example, an individual might use this approach solely for travel and vacation expenses, particularly if they desire to cut back on discretionary outlays when the stock market performs poorly. That would be a rational choice.

Also note that in each of the charts 4.4 through 4.6, the FP portfolio has a substantial balance remaining after 30 years, while the COLA portfolio, by definition, has dwindled to zero. Thus, the FP account could be viewed as having a secondary purpose of providing a legacy for heirs.

Above, we compared the performance of the FP scheme against the COLA scheme by setting IWR equal to the COLA SAFEMAX, to provide a guaranteed 30 years of portfolio longevity for both schemes. Is that a fair comparison of the two? As it turns out, probably not.

Consider Figure 4.8, which computes total withdrawals over 30 years for 10 different retirees using the FP scheme, for IWRs between 3.5% and 8.0%. Not surprisingly, the total withdrawals differ significantly among retirees and are related to the market circumstances they encounter. What is surprising is the inverted U-shape of each curve. That's interesting! For each retiree, there is a "peak" IWR. That is an optimum withdrawal rate that generates the highest cumulative withdrawals. Increasing or decreasing the IWR from this optimum rate results in lower total withdrawals on either side of the peak.

Figure 4.8 Cumulative 30-year withdrawals vs. IWR (FP scheme) (10 retirees). Tax-advantaged account, FP scheme, 40 years longevity, seven asset classes, 55%/40%/5% stocks/bonds/cash.

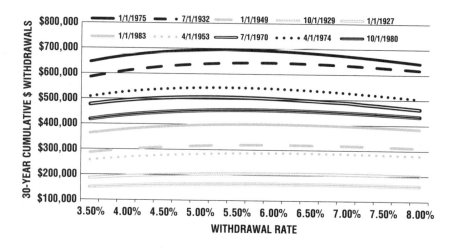

Also note that peak total withdrawals occur between 5.0% WR and 6.25% WR for all retirees. Thus, in our earlier comparisons, we were not fair to the FP withdrawal scheme if we used a withdrawal rate outside of this range. To rectify this error, let's re-compute a few of our charts.

Figure 4.9 reproduces our comparison for the 1 January 1975 retiree in Figure 4.5 with one important difference: we assume an IWR of 5.75% for the FP scheme, while retaining the original 10.0% IWR for the COLA scheme. Even though we reduced the FP withdrawal rate from 10% to 5.75%, the total withdrawals have swelled by about 20% to more than $693,000. How's that for a counterintuitive result?! Furthermore, the total FP withdrawals are quite close to those of the COLA scheme. Best of all, the FP portfolio still has a balance of over $770,000 left at the end of 30 years to fund withdrawals for many years after that time!

Figure 4.9   Annual withdrawals for FP and COLA schemes (1 January 1975 retiree) (IWR = 10.0% for COLA, 5.75% for FP). Tax-advantaged account, 30 years longevity, 55%/40%/5% stocks/ bonds/cash.

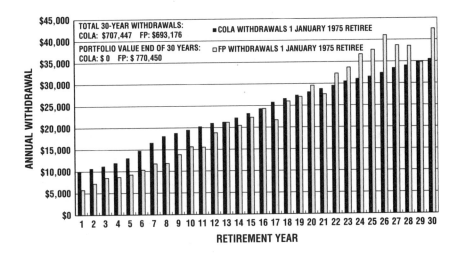

Offsetting these advantages is the much lower annual income the FP scheme produces in the first half of retirement. True, income at the back end of retirement is higher, but that is usually when it is less needed. Overall, the FP scheme does poorly to establish a consistent lifestyle.

Let's convert one more of our earlier charts. Figure 4.10 presents the reconfigured data for the 1 October 1968 retiree from Figure 4.4. The FP IWR has now been raised from 4.7% to 5.75%. This turns out to have a negligible effect on total withdrawals; they are still considerably less than under the COLA scheme. However, annual income has been redistributed, with higher withdrawals in the early years and lower withdrawals in the later years. The 30-year balance has been substantially reduced.

Figure 4.10 Annual withdrawals for FP and COLA schemes (1 October 1968 retiree) (IWR = 4.7% for COLA, 5.75% for FP). Tax-advantaged account, 30 years longevity, 55%40%/5% stocks/bonds/cash.

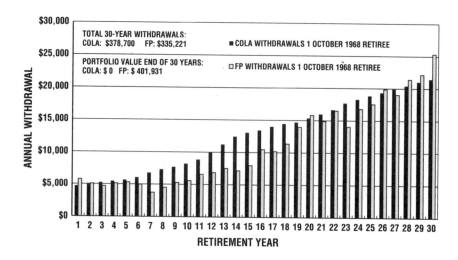

Overall, it is questionable whether using optimized withdrawal rates for the FP scheme produces much value. At best, total withdrawals approach, but are still less than those of the COLA scheme. Annual income also gets shifted in a manner that may not suit the individual retiree.

As a final observation, optimizing the FP IWR is a tricky proposition. For one, the relationship between IWR and cumulative withdrawals is not linear. That is, a 10% increase in the IWR does not automatically lead to a 10% increase in cumulative withdrawals. Usually, it is far less than 10%. And counterintuitively, increasing the IWR can sometimes lead to lower cumulative withdrawals, and vice versa. This research gives me such a headache sometimes!

As a last word on this topic, although the FP scheme may appeal for some of the reasons cited earlier, I believe other approaches, such as the "decision rules" espoused by Jonathan Guyton and discussed below, probably accomplish its objectives more efficiently.

4.4 "FRONT-LOADED" WITHDRAWAL SCHEME

Next, we'll discuss a withdrawal scheme that I believe will be much more useful for retirees than the FA or FP schemes. It reflects a conviction that many retirees would prefer to spend more heavily early on items such as travel, vacations, etc., while their energy levels are still high, and then cut back on those expenses later in retirement. I call that concept "front-loading" (FL) expenses, hence the name of this withdrawal scheme.

In his 1998 book, *The Prosperous Retirement: Guide to the New Reality*, CFP® Michael K. Stein presented a three-phase model for retirement expenses:

Active Phase: The retiree lives an active lifestyle, including travel, social activities, and sports. This phase lasts through the mid-70s. Expenses are about equal to pre-retirement expenses.

Passive Phase: Lifestyle slows down. The need for income declines as activities decline. This phase lasts to the mid-80s.

Final Phase: Retirees experience declining energy and physical and mental health. Substantial expenses are associated with medical and nursing care. This phase lasts till death.

In my 2006 book, I analyzed this approach by using three phases with varying withdrawal levels driven by adjustments to inflation. Upon reflection, I consider that method too complex and confusing. For this book, I will use just two phases, Phase 1 (10 years long) and Phase 2 (the remainder of retirement), during both of which withdrawals will increase with inflation. However, withdrawals will be subject to an arbitrary reduction in the eleventh year at the beginning of Phase 2. Thus, there will be what I call a "withdrawal cliff" at the start of Phase 2.

Let's think more about how to analyze this. If Phase 1 withdrawals begin at the COLA SAFEMAX level and then decline in Phase 2, it is clear there is no problem with portfolio longevity, as total withdrawals will always be less than in the SAFEMAX portfolio. As a matter of definition, the portfolio will always have a positive balance after 30 years instead of the zero balance we strive for. That contradicts our intention to spend as much as possible during retirement.

To make the analysis more useful, I'll consider only scenarios in which Phase 1 withdrawals begin **above** the SAFEMAX level, which, if continued unabated, would inevitably cause the portfolio to fail before the end of its planning horizon. We shall then compute how much reduction is required in Phase 2 to permit the portfolio to last its intended life. In that sense, the size of the "cliff" becomes our most crucial variable.

Figure 4.11 shows the results of these computations for three sample retirees ("the usual suspects"): the 31 October 1968 retiree (low SAFEMAX),

Figure 4.11 "Cliff %" required for given IWR, front-loaded scheme (three retirees). Tax-advantaged account, 30 years longevity, 55%/40%/5% stocks/bonds/cash.

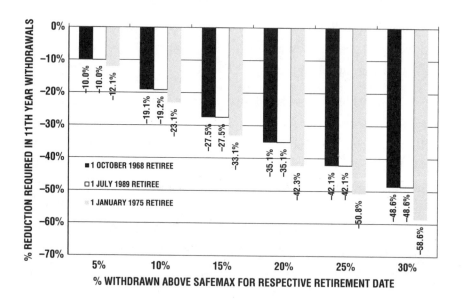

the 1 July 1989 retiree (average SAFEMAX), and the 1 January 1975 retiree (high SAFEMAX.) For each retiree, I've computed the "cliff" for each of six different initial withdrawal rates (i.e., 5% greater than SAFEMAX, 10% greater than SAFEMAX, 15% than SAFEMAX, etc.). For each initial withdrawal rate, the cliff is the percentage by which withdrawals must be reduced in the eleventh year to sustain the portfolio for its intended longevity, in this example, 30 years.

I don't know if we can learn much in this case by comparing one retiree's numbers with another. What is immediately evident, though, for each retiree, is that the cliff percentage is always higher than the corresponding IWR percentage increase over SAFEMAX. For example, at the far left of the chart, all three retirees begin retirement by withdrawing 5% more than the COLA scheme SAFEMAX would dictate. Yet, for each of them, the cliff percentage is considerably higher, 10% or more.

Furthermore, as the percentage withdrawn above SAFEMAX increases, the cliff becomes increasingly steep for all three retirees. In fact, as a very crude rule of thumb, one might postulate that the cliff percentage is roughly *double* the percentage by which the initial withdrawal rate exceeds SAFEMAX. Oh, good, another rule!

Note that this conclusion applies to only this group of three retirees under the assumptions made with respect to each of the other eight Elements. As we shall see in Case Study #3 in Chapter 12, changing the assumptions will alter this apparent rule of thumb. Once again, rules don't always rule!

Let's allow that "doubling rule" to sink in for a moment. To cite an example (from Figure 4.11), an initial withdrawal rate 15% above SAFEMAX leads to a cliff of about 30% for all retirees. That's a hefty drop! To frame it in dollar terms, if an individual with a SAFEMAX of about 7% (like the 1 July 1989 retiree) chooses to withdraw at a rate of 15% above SAFEMAX, their first-year withdrawal from a $100,000 portfolio will be approximately $8,050.

When they reach the eleventh year, that will have to be cut to the inflation-adjusted equivalent of $5,635.

I'm certainly not claiming it's unfeasible; I can easily imagine discretionary spending that could be cut drastically after 10 years. I'm just asserting that front-loading one's expenses in retirement demands that one have a keen awareness of the magnitude of the changes that eventually must be made in the eleventh year to keep the portfolio viable. Forewarned is forearmed!

4.5 PERFORMANCE-BASED WITHDRAWAL SCHEMES

As you may recall from our earlier discussion, in the early years of "sustainable withdrawal" research (and, in fact, up until quite recently), there was no reliable, fact-based method for selecting withdrawal rates from the broad spectrum that had been historically observed. Thus, many retirees (and advisors) simply opted for the "worst-case" scenario (the "4.7% rule") because it had worked in all previous historical environments. However, as we have learned, that was not an entirely satisfactory approach, as it often left the retiree with substantial account balances at the end of retirement and a sense of regret at not having been more aggressive in their spending.

This dilemma logically led to experimentation with withdrawal schemes that adjusted the withdrawal rate based on the portfolio's performance. The goal was to utilize higher withdrawal rates than the "worst-case" scenario when circumstances were favorable. This idea makes sense, as strong portfolio performance, particularly early in retirement, often leads to higher withdrawal rates.

In his seminal 2004 article, "Decision Rules and Portfolio Management for Retirees: Is the Safe Initial Withdrawal Rate Too Safe?" Minneapolis-based financial advisor Jonathan Guyton pioneered the concept of "decision rules" for managing retirement portfolios. His goal was maximization of the "safe" withdrawal rate, partly by funding withdrawals with the proceeds of the sale of a portion of asset classes that outperformed the prior year. He also explored the benefits of a rule that mandated that no withdrawals be increased the year after the portfolio has a "down" year. These are both characteristics of a "performance-based" withdrawal scheme.

Guyton followed up on his initial work, coauthoring with William J. Klinger a paper titled "Decision Rules and Maximum Initial Withdrawal Rates." That paper introduced the concept of "financial guardrails," which are rules activated when market conditions cause the withdrawal rate to rise or fall significantly. Quoting from the Conclusions of that paper, "Our analysis using Monte Carlo simulations supports the conclusion that the application of a few simple but powerful decision rules can significantly increase maximum initial withdrawal rates while virtually eliminating the possibility that a 'perfect storm' could cause a retiree to run out of money." This idea is a further enhancement of a performance-based withdrawal scheme.

Although I will not undertake a detailed analysis of Guyton and Klinger's approach in this book, their methodology is worth considering. Their emphasis on capital preservation is appealing to me.

In my 2006 book, I proposed a "Floor and Ceiling (F&C)" scheme that allowed withdrawals to rise and fall within prescribed limits, driven by investment performance. I gave the concept a few pages in the book, then forgot about it for the next 18 years. When I was writing this book, I developed a renewed sense of appreciation for its virtues. Its features may appeal to retirees searching for a withdrawal scheme that satisfies their natural urge to cut back on expenses when stocks are getting hammered. Let's take a closer look at this withdrawal scheme.

The F&C scheme is a variation of the FP scheme, as it also requires withdrawals to fluctuate as a fixed percentage of portfolio value. However, the F&C "ceiling" specifies a maximum real (inflation-adjusted) dollar withdrawal, which, once attained, is never allowed to be exceeded. This ceiling is expressed as a percentage above the first year's withdrawal. Concomitantly, a "floor" is also specified, which sets a minimum real dollar withdrawal, which, once attained, is never allowed to decline further. The floor is also expressed as a percentage below the first year's withdrawal.

Together, the floor and the ceiling act as "governors" on the potentially unbridled fluctuation of dollar withdrawals experienced under the naked FP scheme, providing them some stability. Although the concept of SAFEMAX does not apply to the FP scheme, as it never completely exhausts the portfolio, it does apply to the F&C scheme, as exhaustion is a possibility.

Before explaining this any further, let's examine a visualization. Figure 4.12 illustrates how the F&C scheme performed for the 1 April 1926 retiree. I've chosen this date for fun; the chart zigs and zags more than any other I am aware of, boldly illustrating the "floor and ceiling" concept. Yes, this is a weird-looking chart!

To create this chart, we must first specify some parameters. We arbitrarily set the floor withdrawal at 10% less than the real value of the first year's withdrawal. This ensures that, adjusted for inflation, withdrawals will never be more than 10% less than those of the first year. We could have chosen any percentage, but 10% seems like a reasonable amount to cut back one's lifestyle to preserve capital temporarily. More would be painful for most people; less probably would not create a significant benefit.

Next, we establish the ceiling withdrawal at 10% above the real value of the first year's withdrawal. We do so in the hope that this will provide an opportunity to make higher withdrawals than provided for by the

Figure 4.12   Real withdrawals for "floor and ceiling" scheme (1 April 1926 retiree). Tax-advantaged account, 30 years longevity, 55%/40%/5% stocks/bonds/cash, 9.37% IWR, floor −10%, ceiling +10%.

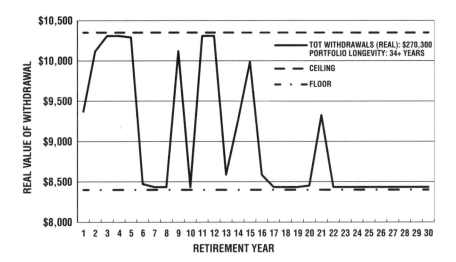

COLA scheme. Selecting more than 20% seems greedy and might threaten the portfolio's longevity. As with the floor, a lower percentage hardly seems worth the effort.

Finally, we need to specify the initial withdrawal rate (IWR) for the F&C scheme. The COLA scheme SAFEMAX for the 1 April 1926 retiree is 9.37%. Since we'll eventually be comparing the outcome of the FC scheme with that of the COLA scheme, let's use that percentage as the IWR for the F&C scheme as well so that we're comparing "apples with apples."

Returning to Figure 4.12, we are struck by the volatility of annual withdrawals. This is mainly due to the investment environment for the 1 April 1926 retiree, who experienced no less than six negative portfolio returns in their first 15 years, a highly unusual occurrence. In a total of five years, the retiree had to cut withdrawals substantially, and in five other years was able to enjoy a significant increase in withdrawals. There's not a lot of stability in this scenario.

Figure 4.13   Real withdrawals for three withdrawal schemes (4/1/1926 retiree). Tax-advantaged account, 30 years longevity (for COLA scheme), 55%/40%/5% stocks/bonds/cash.

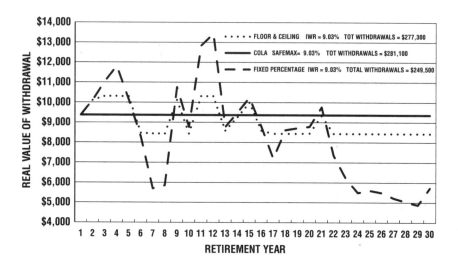

Let's provide a meatier context for the above discussion. Figure 4.13 displays the results of applying the COLA and FP schemes to the same 1 April 1926 retiree, alongside the F&C scheme from Figure 4.12. For consistency, all three schemes employ the same IWR of 9.37%. Note that because of the broader vertical scale of Figure 4.13, the apparent wild gyrations of the F&C scheme in Figure 4.12 now seem relatively tame. As usual, it's a matter of perspective.

Note that the withdrawal amounts that appear in Figure 4.13 are expressed in "real" dollars: they are adjusted for inflation. This provided the most reliable measure of the "spending power" wielded by the retiree at any time during retirement. Declining real withdrawals suggests that the retiree is losing purchasing power, thus suffering a decline in lifestyle.

One observation that should be made concerning Figure 4.13 is that the F&C portfolio lasted more than 34 years at the given IWR. That's more than four years longer than the planning horizon of the COLA scheme and might be considered a hidden benefit of the F&C scheme.

At the outset, it's apparent that the big loser in the "withdrawal derby" is the Fixed Percentage scheme. The pressure of multiple years with negative portfolio returns eventually sends it into the cellar. Its 30-year total of real withdrawals is the lowest by far of the three schemes. All the weaknesses I mentioned in my earlier analysis are in full evidence.

The best performer, but only by a modest margin, is the COLA scheme. Because each year's withdrawals rise with inflation, this scheme appears as a straight line on the chart. Its 30-year total real withdrawals are at the head of the class, more than $281,000. "Old dependable" made its mark with class.

In between these two, but performing with distinction, is the F&C scheme. It's true that its cumulative real withdrawals of $270,300 trailed that of the COLA scheme, but only by a few percentage points. What is not evident from the chart is that the F&C scheme outlasted the COLA scheme by a year and a half. From another angle, if we were to use the 30-year SAFEMAX for the F&C scheme, its 30-year real withdrawals would have been virtually in a dead heat with COLA. In this retirement scenario, there is very little to choose between them.

Some might criticize the choice of the 1 April 1926 retirement date as being unfair and not representative of the 100-year record. I agree. Let's use the date of 1 January 1983 instead – shortly after the start of one of the greatest stock and bond bull markets on record – and run these three ponies around the track again.

Figure 4.14 shows the results. The FP line is probably sufficient to make all the handicappers give up on this pony. Although it showed promise early, rising briefly about the COLA line, FP soon ran out of gas and sank into oblivion. Again, it came in last, this time lengths behind. "'Nuff" said about it.

Figure 4.14   Real withdrawals for three withdrawal schemes (January 1 1983 retiree). Tax-advantaged account, 30 years longevity, 55%/40%/5% stocks/bonds/cash.

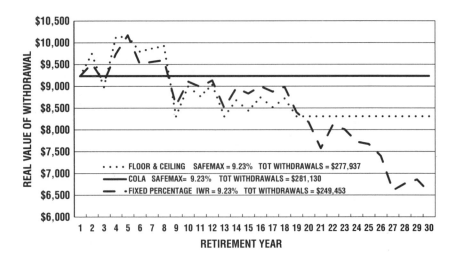

The performance of the F&C scheme was superior to that of the FP, particularly in the last 10 years of retirement, when it avoided the steep dip experienced by the FP scheme. It also lasted about a year and a half longer than the COLA scheme. However, the −5% loss in the eighth year of retirement sent F&C into a tailspin, from which it never really recovered.

The clear winner, once again, is the COLA scheme, which generated the highest total withdrawals over the 30 years and required no wrenching adjustments to retiree lifestyle. It navigated all markets, up and down, and although its lead over the F&C method is not overwhelming, it is definitive.

In summary, F&C offers some value to investors who prefer to cut back on withdrawals during significant stock market downturns. It preserves capital, with the added bonus of extending the portfolio's longevity.

What is my take on Performance-Based Schemes, then, overall? I believe they offer value for those willing to accept the accompanying potential reductions in their annual withdrawals. They also provide a rational means for dealing with market circumstances that are literally "off the charts" and have no historical precedent.

However, I still believe that the "two-factor" (CPI and CAPE) method I have developed recently offers the best chance for superior withdrawal performance. It puts the retiree on the right track to begin with and can accommodate unexpected or unprecedented market conditions through ongoing monitoring and "mid-course corrections."

Then again, I'm probably biased. Hopefully, the contents of this book provide sufficient rationale to justify that apparent prejudice.

4.6   DAVID BLANCHETT'S RETIREMENT "SMILE"

David Blanchett, a leading retirement researcher and prolific author on the subject, challenged the notion of inflation-adjusted spending (i.e., the COLA withdrawal model) by retirees in a 2014 article (see Appendix B). He cited a "growing body of empirical research" that revealed that "retiree expenditures tend to decrease both upon and during retirement." He referred to this disparity as a "retirement consumption puzzle."

David's analysis confirms that retirement spending does decline in inflation-adjusted terms. He concludes: "The actual changes in real retirement spending create a 'retirement spending smile' whereby the expenditures increase at a faster rate (although these are still negative) for relatively younger and relatively older retirees. The 'smile' can likely be attributed to the fact younger retirees are better able to travel and enjoy retirement, while older retirees incur higher relative medical expenses. The overall changes in real spending, though, are clearly negative; the only real variation is the extent of the negative change."

Figure 4.15   Real withdrawals for David Blanchett's "retirement smile" (conceptual) 20-year time horizon.

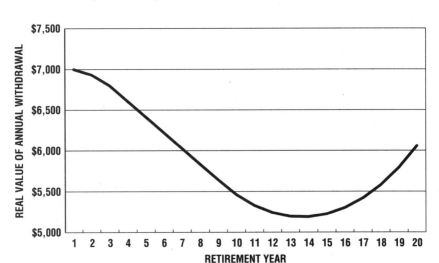

The "smile" David refers to is the shape of the retirement spending curve, illustrated in Figure 4.15. This figure is not intended to precisely represent his data, but rather serve as a conceptual aid.

David further states in his paper, "The fact that spending tends to decrease in real terms during retirement may lead to suboptimal retirement consumption. Retirees may be better served by planning on spending more early in retirement (and saving more for later in retirement) than assuming some constant inflation-adjusted amount. Spending more early in retirement also allows retirees the ability to spend money on things they may be unable to enjoy later in retirement as health declines."

This comment suggests an approach to retirement spending somewhat akin to the "Front-Loaded" withdrawal scheme we discussed in Section 4.4. The main difference between the two is that he envisions expenses gradually and continually changing during retirement, while the FL scheme embodies a cliff-like reduction in expenses during Year #11. In that sense, the FL scheme might be considered a "broken-tooth smile."

I find David's ruminations on this topic fascinating. If there is enough interest from readers, I will attempt to model his withdrawal scheme in future editions of this book or provide downloadable charts on my website.

As a final note, for practical reasons, I couldn't escape David's "retirement smile," even if I wanted to. I'm reminded of it every time I receive a package from Amazon!

No connection between the two, of course.

CHAPTER 5

ELEMENT #2: PLANNING HORIZON

5.1 LIFE EXPECTANCY AND PLANNING HORIZON

Your "planning horizon" is the length of time you specify that you will be withdrawing money from your retirement account. It's closely related to, but not identical to, your life expectancy.

Life expectancy can be a thorny subject. For some individuals, it may be difficult to contemplate for emotional reasons, as it forces them to confront their mortality. However, establishing a "planning horizon" is essential to developing a rational withdrawal plan. If you find it challenging to grapple with the subject yourself, whatever the reason, perhaps you could enlist the services of a friend or loved one to help select it for you.

Regardless of how you proceed, it's vital to incorporate a "margin of error" into your selection of a planning horizon. All the withdrawal schemes we have discussed so far assume that you'll spend your last penny as you exhale your last breath at the end of the planning horizon. Few of us can achieve such precise timing! I recommend, for safety, that you choose a planning horizon substantially longer than you expect to live. Of necessity, this implies a lower withdrawal rate. Consider this approach a form of insurance for an unexpectedly (and hopefully welcome) long life, and the reduction in withdrawal rate a form of "insurance premium."

What would be the ideal margin of error? I believe at least 5 years, but 10 years sounds much safer. After all, how accurately can we forecast how long we'll live? Not much better than we can predict the weather 10 years from today. Just as we use investment diversification because we can't accurately foresee the performance of individual asset classes, so we should conservatively estimate our planning horizon.

5.2 UNIVERSAL SAFEMAX VS. PLANNING HORIZON (STANDARD CONFIGURATION)

Let's examine how, historically, SAFEMAX has varied with changes in the planning horizon. For our test case, let's begin with our "worst case" 1 October 1968 retiree. Thus, we'll look at variations in the Universal SAFEMAX for various planning horizons. We'll also use almost all of the assumptions of our "standard configuration" (a fixed 55%/40%/5% stock/bond/cash allocation, the stock asset classes equally weighted, a tax-advantaged account, annual rebalancing, zero ending value, etc.). The only assumption we will vary, of course, will be the planning horizon.

Figure 5.1 SAFEMAX vs. planning horizon (10/1/1968 retiree) (low SAFEMAX). Tax-advantaged account, 55%/40%/5% stocks/bonds/cash, seven asset classes.

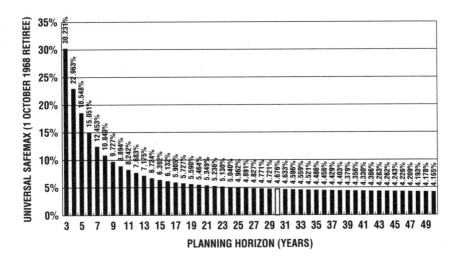

Figure 5.1 shows how the SAFEMAX for the 1 October 1968 retiree varies for planning horizons from 3 to 50 years (including less than a three-year horizon significantly distorts the chart's scale). Near the center of the chart is our "standard" 30-year longevity, with the familiar 4.7% "worst case" withdrawal rate, or Universal SAFEMAX.

For very short planning horizons, SAFEMAX is very high; for horizons of eight years or less, it reaches double digits. This is not surprising, as for a short planning horizon, even if it includes a bear market, there is not enough time for low returns (and possibly high inflation) to wreak significant damage on the portfolio. Plenty of capital will almost always be available to withdraw at high rates.

As we move from left to right on the chart and the planning horizon increases, SAFEMAX decreases. At first, the declines are very steep, but as the planning horizon lengthens, the declines become shallower and shallower until the curve looks virtually flat. Although it's not shown on the chart, beyond a horizon of 65 years, SAFEMAX remains virtually unchanged at approximately 4.1%. This should prove reassuring to those of you planning one hundred or more years in retirement. Gosh, that's a lot of pickleball!

In my 2006 book, I referred to individuals with such very long retirement horizons as "Methuselah retirees." In practice, even among the early-retiring FIRE group (Financially Independent, Retire Early), very few individuals will today enjoy a retirement as long as 65 years. However, this may change as medical technology advances, and the "Methuselah retiree" may become more commonplace. Let's hope we'll all be prepared for the psychological hurdles of living for 150 years!

5.3 SAFEMAX VS. PLANNING HORIZON (OTHER SAMPLE RETIREES)

So far, we've seen that for the 1 October 1968 retiree, SAFEMAX decreases steadily as the length of the planning horizon increases, and finally approaches (but never quite reaches) a "floor" for very long planning horizons. In mathematics, this is called an "asymptote," but I didn't mean to spoil your day with jargon. For purposes of comparison, Figures 5.2 and 5.3 present the same information for two retirees we have used before: the 1 July 1989 retiree, with a historically "average" SAFEMAX of about 7.1%, and the 1 January 1975, who enjoyed a "high" SAFEMAX of 10.0%.

The most obvious conclusion from examining the three charts is that they all have the same general shape: SAFEMAX declines from left to right as the planning horizon lengthens, at first very steeply, and then ever more gradually, and eventually approaches a "floor" value beyond which SAFEMAX is essentially unchanged for ultra-long planning horizons.

Figure 5.2   SAFEMAX vs. planning horizon (1 July 1989 retiree) (average SAFEMAX). Tax-advantaged account, 55%/40%/5% stocks/bonds/cash, seven asset classes.

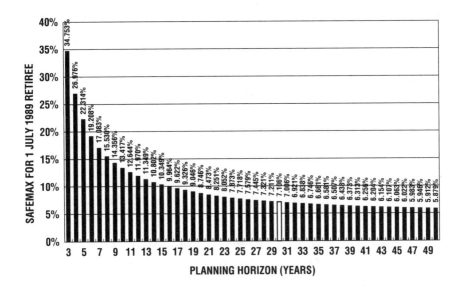

Figure 5.3   SAFEMAX vs. planning horizon (1 January 1975 retiree) (high SAFEMAX). Tax-advantaged account, 55%/40%/5% stocsks/bonds/cash, seven asset classes.

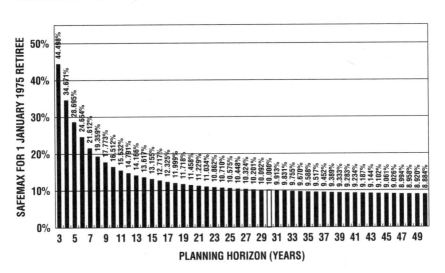

The specific SAFEMAX values are different for each retiree, of course. For every planning horizon, the 1 January 1975 retiree always has the highest SAFEMAX, the 1 October 1968 retiree always has the lowest SAFEMAX, and the 1 July 1989 retiree always lies somewhere in between. There are no exceptions to this observation. The circumstances that gave rise to a different SAFEMAX for each of these three retirees influence all of their retirement portfolios consistently.

There is also a difference in the "floor," or lowest SAFEMAX, for each of these retirees and when it is very nearly achieved, as summarized in Table 5.1.

Table 5.1   SAFEMAX for very long planning horizons (three retirees). Standard configuration of Elements assumed, except for planning horizon.

Retirement Date	30-Year SAFEMAX	Floor SAFEMAX	Horizon for Floor SAFEMAX	Floor SAFEMAX/ 30-Year SAFEMAX
31 October 1968	4.68%	4.10%	65 years	88%
1 July 1989	7.11%	5.38%	90 years	76%
1 January 1975	10.00%	8.20%	100 years	82%

It appears that the higher the overall SAFEMAX for a retiree, the longer it takes to achieve a stable "floor" at very long planning horizons. Furthermore, the floor SAFEMAX for each retiree is between 75% and 90% of the 30-year SAFEMAX. I am uncertain if there is any discernible pattern in the last statistic.

5.4   CONCLUSION

We can make the general statement that SAFEMAX will decline with a lengthening planning horizon for each retiree. As with much of my research, no quick-and-dirty "rule" emerges, expressing the relationship between SAFEMAX and the planning horizon for all retirees. Eventually, SAFEMAX will approach a "floor value," which remains effectively constant for all longer planning horizons. But to get the specifics for any retiree, one must "run the numbers."

We will revisit this topic in the next chapter.

CHAPTER 6

ELEMENT #3: TAXABLE VS. NON-TAXABLE PORTFOLIOS

S o far, we've examined SAFEMAX only for "tax-advantaged" (tax-free and tax-deferred) portfolios. Of course, some investors may choose to fund their retirement by withdrawing primarily from a taxable portfolio. In this chapter, we'll examine the effect of taxation on SAFEMAX.

6.1 MY INITIAL DILEMMA

At the beginning of my research in the early 1990s, I faced several critical questions about accounting for income tax effects in retirement withdrawals. Should I include the taxes on withdrawals from IRA accounts in my computation of SAFEMAX? Or should I ignore the impact of income taxes altogether, even in taxable accounts, and just assume the retiree possessed another source of wealth that could fund tax payments?

After much deliberation, I answered "No" to those two questions. I'm glad I did! Including taxes in the way those questions suggest would have significantly complicated my methodology and muddied my findings. *Instead, I adopted the principle that regardless of tax status, all accounts would only pay taxes on internally generated income. No consideration would be given to income taxes arising from a withdrawal, as from an IRA account.* I call this the "out of sight, out of mind" approach to income taxes.

Naturally, a tax liability will be created if an investor makes withdrawals from a traditional IRA account. That tax liability must be paid from another source, or income taxes must be withheld from the distribution. In either case, the income taxes become an expense that becomes a budget item, as part of an overall financial plan. But that is beyond the purview of my work.

Adopting this approach allows me to treat all accounts in the same manner. For me, tax-advantaged accounts are just like taxable accounts; they just happen to have a zero tax rate. I spend most of my time writing about tax-advantaged accounts because the lack of taxes makes them more straightforward to deal with, and many retirees use them as the primary source of income during retirement. However, our analysis would be incomplete without examining how SAFEMAX varies for taxable accounts.

6.2 INVESTMENT CHARACTERISTICS

Let's discuss how I represent investments in my spreadsheet models. Each of the seven asset classes I use is represented in the portfolio by a single investment, which has the characteristics of a "fund," i.e., a mutual fund or an exchange-traded fund. Each fund tracks precisely the returns for its asset class as specified in my historical database; the fund is assumed to have zero operating expenses. As it turns out, this is very close to the current nature of real-life index funds.

I assume that each fund pays income and capital gains dividends once annually, at the end of each year. Historical records determine income distributions: for stocks, they are computed from their annual dividend yield, and for bonds and Treasury bills, they are calculated from their yearly interest yield. All income distributions are taxed at ordinary income rates, which of course vary between individuals.

Income distributions occur in all asset classes except US Small-Company stocks and US Micro-Cap stocks, which, in my historical database, pay zero dividends. This accurately reflects reality, as most smaller companies use their profits to reinvest in their business and do not pay dividends to shareholders.

The determination of capital gains distributions is a bit more complex. My historical database's annual "capital appreciation return" for each asset class determines capital gains each year. At the end of each year, a predetermined fraction of accumulated capital gains in each fund is distributed and taxed at capital gains tax rates. This fraction is a variable and can be assigned any value, but I set it arbitrarily at 70% unless otherwise specified. This high fraction, probably greater than that experienced by most real-life funds, assures the portfolio will not accumulate excessive capital gains, which could potentially distort the eventual taxation of those gains.

Capital gains occur in all asset classes except Treasury Bills, which, like cash, is assumed not to enjoy any appreciation. All distributions, whether from income or capital gains, are deemed reinvested in their originating fund at the end of each year, net of any income taxes paid from the distribution.

No capital gains income is generated if an investment is sold (either to fund a withdrawal or to rebalance the portfolio), and therefore, no capital gains tax liability is created. This assumption may be unrealistic and tends to understate capital gains taxes if distributions are a significant fraction of the portfolio value. Still, I felt it was a necessary simplification. Remember, capital gains taxes will eventually be paid on all accumulated gains because of the method I described in the prior paragraph.

6.3 SAFEMAX AND PORTFOLIO TAX RATES

Ordinary income and capital appreciation income tax rates are variables in my spreadsheet models and can be assigned any value. Once values are assigned to each of these, one may also compute an "overall portfolio tax rate (PTR)," which is merely the sum of all portfolio income taxes paid divided by total portfolio investment income. PTR is the most critical parameter, as what counts for the computation of SAFEMAX is the total dollars a portfolio pays to cover income taxes generated by investment income. The calculation of SAFEMAX doesn't distinguish between dollars paid for ordinary income taxes and dollars paid for capital gains taxes.

Figure 6.1 illustrates, for the 1 October 1968 retiree, how SAFEMAX varies with PTR. At the far left is our familiar 4.7% Universal SAFEMAX, for a tax-advantaged portfolio (i.e., a portfolio with a 0% tax rate). As we move right on the chart, PTR increases and SAFEMAX decreases. Analysis shows this is an almost perfect straight-line relationship which can be modeled by a straightforward formula.

**Figure 6.1   SAFEMAX vs. overall tax rate (10/1/1968 retiree).
Standard configuration, seven asset classes.**

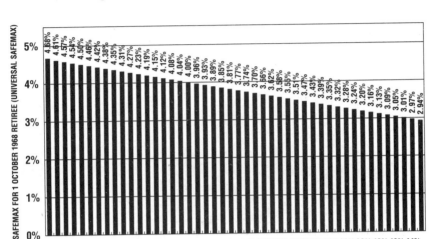

Portfolio tax rates have a dramatic effect on SAFEMAX. For example, increasing the PTR from 0% to 17% causes SAFEMAX to decline from 4.7% to 4.0%, a reduction of almost 15%. There's a new "4.7% rule" for you! (Please don't tell anyone I said that.)

Figures 6.2 and 6.3 illustrate the same information for two other retirement dates, 1 January 1975 (high SAFEMAX) and 1 July 1989 (average SAFEMAX). Not surprisingly, although the values of SAFEMAX differ from retiree to retiree, the straight-line relationship between SAFEMAX and PTR appears to be maintained for all retirees. However, the "slope" of the line differs from retiree to retiree. In particular, SAFEMAX declined far more steeply for the 1 January 1975 retiree than for the other two retirees, losing more than half its value across the breadth of the chart. This is probably not surprising, as the 1 January 1975 portfolio generated much higher returns and thus far more investment income than the other two retirees, therefore increasing its sensitivity to higher portfolio tax rates.

Figure 6.2   SAFEMAX vs. overall tax rate (1 January 1975 retiree).
Standard configuration, seven asset classes.

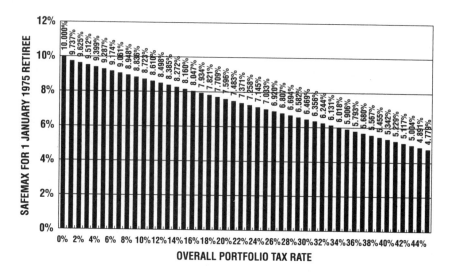

Figure 6.3   SAFEMAX vs. overall tax rate (1 July 1989 retiree).
Standard configuration, seven asset classes.

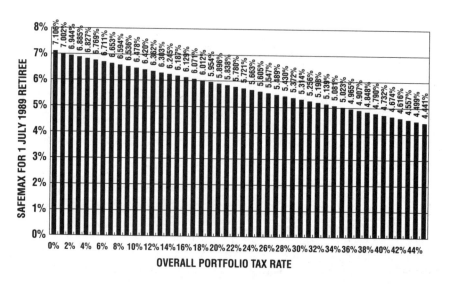

For all retirees across long planning horizons, portfolios generated roughly 30% of their gross income from dividends and interest and 70% from capital gains. Since capital gains tax rates are generally lower than ordinary income tax rates, our retirement portfolios are reasonably tax-efficient.

Unfortunately, I've not discovered a theoretical means by which similar SAFEMAX/PTR curves can be constructed for other retirees based on some simple equation. Perhaps that will one day be revealed. For now, unfortunately, to get similar charts for other retirees requires "running the numbers." As an approximation, however, I recommend you use one of the three charts in this chapter, depending on whether your status may be described as "low SAFEMAX" (below 6%), "medium SAFEMAX" (between 6% and 8%), or "high SAFEMAX" (above 8%). For now, you can interpolate between the charts for intermediate values of SAFEMAX. Ultimately I intend to post additional charts on my website for greater accuracy.

6.4 WHICH PTR DO I USE FOR MY PORTFOLIO?

Now that we've understood how SAFEMAX varies with the portfolio tax rate, how do you apply that to your situation? In particular, what tax rate do you use to determine SAFEMAX for your taxable portfolio?

As we all know from bitter experience, computing one's income taxes can be complex, given multiple tax brackets, the distinction between different kinds of income (such as ordinary income and capital gains), and the diversity of deductions, exemptions, and tax credits. Multiple authorities can also tax federal, state, and local income.

Complicating matters further is that your retirement investment portfolio may only generate a portion of your taxable income. You may also derive taxable income from employment, real estate rentals, Social Security, pension benefits, annuity income, limited partnerships, etc.

Rather than being drawn into even more complexity by attempting a precise computation of your personal PTR, I recommend you simply compute your average income tax rate and use that as the basis for computing SAFEMAX for your portfolio. This computation involves no more than dividing your total income tax liability for the last year (from all sources – federal, state, and local) by your total taxable income. Your tax advisor should be able to do this for you with little difficulty.

This is not a perfect solution, but no such animal exists to solve this problem. The existence of multiple income tax brackets makes it virtually impossible to assign a precise tax liability to each of your sources of taxable income. As Warren Buffett has said, it is more important to be approximately correct than precisely wrong.

CHAPTER 7

ELEMENT #4: LEAVING A LEGACY TO YOUR HEIRS

I frequently assume in my research that the portfolio's value at the end of the planning horizon will be precisely zero. Aside from the unlikeliness of this outcome – which is why I recommend adopting a planning horizon with a margin of error – you might prefer to leave a balance in your account and pass it to your heirs. This inheritance, or "legacy," must be specified in the planning process so that the chosen SAFEMAX will reflect it. This chapter will explore the magnitude of those adjustments for tax-deferred and taxable accounts.

7.1 SAFEMAX VS. LEGACY FOR THE STANDARD CONFIGURATION

Let's begin our analysis, as we often do, with the low-SAFEMAX 1 October 1968 retiree. Figure 7.1 examines the effects of specifying a legacy (final account balance at the end of 30 years) of various dollar amounts on SAFEMAX. Note that the legacy is expressed in nominal or non-inflation-adjusted dollars.

At the far left of the chart is our "standard configuration" portfolio, assuming no legacy and associated with a SAFEMAX of about 4.7%. As we move to the right on the chart, the amount of the legacy increases. It's evident, and no surprise, that as the legacy amount increases, SAFEMAX declines. For example, to leave a legacy of $200,000 or twice the nominal value of the original portfolio, the retiree must accept a SAFEMAX of 4.26%. That's about 11% less than the zero-legacy SAFEMAX.

Figure 7.1 SAFEMAX vs. legacy (1 October 1968 retiree) ($100,000 begin value). Standard configuration, seven asset classes.

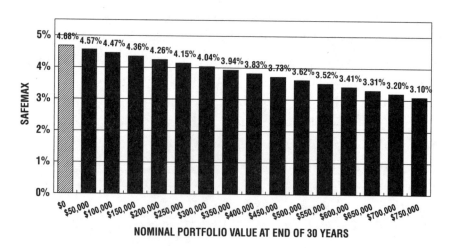

Is leaving a legacy worth such a substantial reduction in SAFEMAX? That's a question only you can answer. If you can live comfortably with a lower withdrawal amount, it might well be acceptable.

7.2 SAFEMAX VS. REAL AND NOMINAL LEGACY

Of course, after 30 years, inflation has whittled away at the value of the legacy, and $200,000 is worth far less than it would have been at the beginning of retirement. Figure 7.2 re-computes SAFEMAX for the 1 October 1968 retiree for legacies expressed in real, or inflation-adjusted terms to gain a better perspective on this issue. Keep in mind that the 1 October 1968 retiree endured many years of high inflation. The CPI averaged over 7% for their first 10 years of retirement.

Figure 7.2   SAFEMAX vs. real legacy (1 October 1968 retiree) ($100,000 begin value). Standard configuration, seven asset classes.

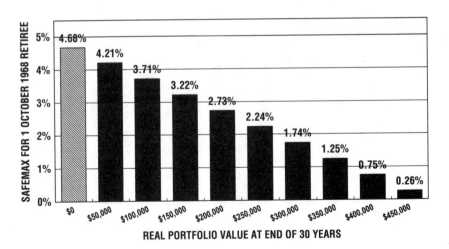

As per the chart, to leave a legacy with the same real value as the $100,000 starting value of their portfolio, this retiree would have had to accept a cut of more than 22% in their annual withdrawals or a reduction in SAFEMAX from about 4.7% to 3.7%. That's twice as severe as for the nominal $100,000 legacy. For higher residual legacies, the cuts are even more draconian. In fact, this retiree couldn't leave a $500,000 real legacy, even if they cut their withdrawals to zero!

7.3 SAFEMAX VS. LEGACY FOR OTHER SAMPLE RETIREES

To further study the legacy issue, Figures 7.3 and 7.4 contain similar information about nominal legacies for two of our other favorite retirees:

Figure 7.3 SAFEMAX vs. legacy (1 January 1975 retiree) ($100,000 begin value). Standard configuration, seven asset classes.

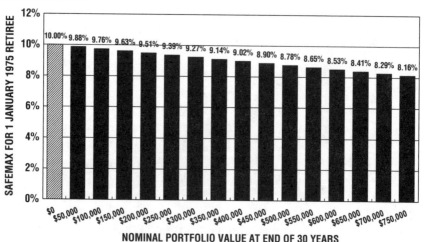

Figure 7.4 SAFEMAX vs. legacy (1 July 1989 retiree) ($100,000 begin value). Standard configuration, seven asset classes.

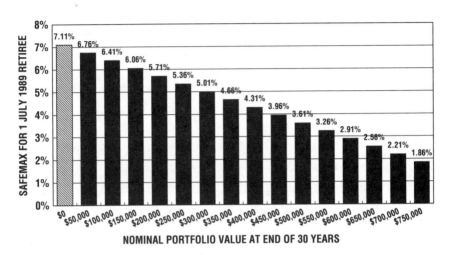

1 January 1975 (high SAFEMAX) and 1 July 1989 (average SAFEMAX). Not surprisingly, both show the same pattern of declining SAFEMAX with increasing legacy.

However, we need to explain an anomaly. Note that SAFEMAX for the 1 July 1989 retiree declines far more rapidly than it does for the other retirees. Although for a $0 legacy it began with a much higher SAFEMAX than the 1968 retiree, at the $750,000 legacy level its SAFEMAX is far lower. It is the lowest SAFEMAX of all three retirees.

How is that possible? With a 7.1% SAFEMAX for a $0 legacy, intermediate between the other two, the 1 July 1989 retiree would have also exhibited intermediate values of SAFEMAX for non-zero legacies. To resolve this conundrum, consult Table 7.1, which presents specific critical facts for each retiree.

Table 7.1   Comparison of 30-year statistics for three retirees.
Standard configuration, seven asset classes.

Retirement Date	SAFEMAX for $0 Legacy	Annualized Inflation	Annualized Portfolio Rate of Return
1 October 1968	4.7%	5.3%	10.9%
1 January 1975	10.0%	4.4%	13.2%
1 July 1989	7.1%	2.5%	8.0%

Note that over 30 years, the 1 July 1989 retiree enjoyed a much lower portfolio rate of return than the other two retirees. It is well below the average of 10.0% for all retirees. The 1989 retiree achieved an "average" SAFEMAX for a $0 legacy only because its inflation rate of 2.5% is well below the average of 3.5% for all retirees. So, concerning SAFEMAX for this retiree, low returns and low inflation offset one another.

When the nominal legacy amount increases above zero, changes in SAFEMAX are most closely associated with changes in the portfolio rate of return. The higher the rate of return, the greater the potential for wealth-building, and the less SAFEMAX declines for a given increase in legacy. This explains our anomaly: the meager returns of the 1 July 1989 retiree are less able to sustain increases in the legacy amount, which causes SAFEMAX to fall faster as legacy increases. It also explains why the 1 January 1975 retiree, with the highest rate of return by far, experienced only modest declines in SAFEMAX as its legacy increased.

The 1968 retiree, with returns intermediate between the other two retirees, saw an intermediate decline in SAFEMAX. However, this applies to a legacy expressed in nominal dollars. When inflation is considered, as in Figure 7.2, the high inflation rate of the 1968 retiree leads to devastating declines in SAFEMAX. From this perspective, the 1 October 1968 retiree is outperformed by the other two.

7.4 CONCLUSION

Although this analysis has established some general patterns, the effects of legacy on SAFEMAX is another one of those topics for which no simple rules of thumb can be devised that apply to all retirees. It is necessary to "run the numbers" on the individual's template year to develop a SAFEMAX for a particular legacy amount. Even then, that estimate of SAFEMAX is subject to the effects of unknowable fluctuations in investment returns and inflation over the planning horizon. These can be addressed by continual monitoring and occasional plan adjustments. As always, nothing is certain in retirement planning.

As with other aspects of my research, I plan to add more "legacy" charts to my website to aid you in your planning. There isn't enough room in this book to include all the required charts. I'm not sure the website can handle it, either, but I'll have a go at it!

Final note: providing for a legacy in your withdrawal plan may offer an unseen benefit. Should you underestimate your life expectancy, the legacy can be used to fund the unexpected length of your retirement. In that sense, it can provide an additional "margin of error" over and above the use of a longer planning horizon (than seems justified by life expectancy). That may disappoint your heirs, but it's better than going hungry, is it not? And green fees aren't getting any cheaper!

CHAPTER 8

ELEMENT #5: ASSET ALLOCATION

8.1 THE SIGNIFICANCE OF ASSET ALLOCATION

Professional money managers often use various financial investments, called "asset classes," to build a diversified investment portfolio. There is a large body of theory and practice to support the soundness of this approach. Asset classes include US Treasury Bills, US Large-Company Stocks, International Developed Market Stocks, Emerging Market Bonds, Precious Metals, Commodities, Real Estate, etc.

Each asset class experiences a range of investment returns over time, some greater and some lesser. The magic of a diversified portfolio arises from the phenomenon that each asset class enjoys peaks and valleys of performance at different times in the economic cycle. As a result, some investments are rising in value while others are falling in value, reducing portfolio volatility and enhancing overall returns. In this sense, a portfolio is greater than the sum of its parts.

The "Asset Allocation" process assigns a specific share of the investment pie to each asset class (it also refers to the finished product). It's a well-studied topic in the investment field and the subject of many books and articles, some of which are listed in the Appendices. In this book, I intend to focus on asset allocation only from the perspective of increasing SAFEMAX without increasing investment risk.

8.2 SAFEMAX VS. ASSET ALLOCATION: A HISTORICAL PERSPECTIVE

The importance of asset allocation in determining withdrawal rates was driven home to me early in my research. A variation of one of the first charts I created appears in Figure 8.1. At the time (1993), I was using only two asset classes in my research: Intermediate-Term US Government Bonds (ITGB) (5–10 years maturity) and US Large-Company Stocks (LCS). This is hardly a diversified portfolio, but I preferred to keep matters simple early on.

Figure 8.1 computes the Universal SAFEMAX for a range of equity allocations for this two-asset portfolio. As you may recall, Universal SAFEMAX is the "worst-case" safe withdrawal rate across all historical retirement dates (the 269 stalwarts in this case). Each bar represents a specific, fixed allocation to LCS; the remainder of the portfolio is allocated to ITGB. To determine the Universal SAFEMAX associated with each allocation, all 269 retirement portfolios were compared to find the one with the lowest SAFEMAX. This became the Universal SAFEMAX

Figure 8.1   Universal SAFEMAX vs. equity allocation (two asset classes) 30-year horizon, tax-advantaged account, two asset classes (US Large-Company stocks and US Intermediate-Term Govt Bonds), through 1 January 1993

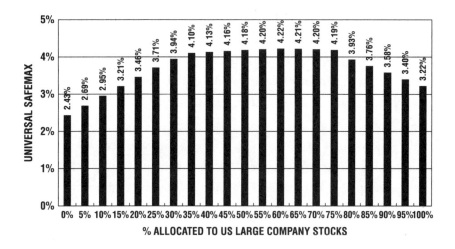

for that specific LCS allocation and was used to establish the height of each allocation bar.

This means that each bar may represent a different retirement date. In fact, all the stock allocations below 35% had their SAFEMAX determined by portfolios initiated in the 1930s and 1940s, when interest rates for bonds were low. One might consider this period a "bond bear market." That meant bond-heavy portfolios suffered low returns in their early years, suppressing withdrawal rates.

Concomitantly, bars for LCS allocations from 35% to 75% all represent portfolios initiated in the 1960s, when stock returns were low and inflation was high. This caused stock-heavy portfolios to generate low overall returns, thereby suppressing withdrawal rates. Finally, at the highest equity allocations, above 75%, all portfolios were initiated on a single date, 1 October 1929. This is just a few weeks before the worst stock market decline of the last one hundred years, which scalped more 90% from stock prices in just three years. Not surprisingly, corresponding withdrawal rates also plummeted.

Note that none of these dates correspond to 1 October 1968, the "worst-case" scenario for our standard configuration, which includes 55% allocated to stocks. This date will appear below when we discuss a seven-asset portfolio, but only for a limited number of allocations. This observation underlines the need to avoid generalizations in this kind of research. Every change in the value of one of the "Elements" can change the withdrawal rate.

As you can see, Figure 8.1 suggests that a withdrawal rate of about 4.2% was optimal for the two-asset portfolio. This is slightly higher than the rate I computed in 1993, as I used a somewhat different method to calculate withdrawals. This chart is probably the source of the term "the 4% rule" (now "the 4.7% rule"), for better or worse, as it's easy to round the 4.2% down to an even 4% for conversational purposes. But don't try to take that 0.2% away from someone in retirement!

Before I move on to the results of my more recent research, I want to point out in Figure 8.1 the "plateau" in SAFEMAX for LCS allocations from 35% to 75%. I found this a fascinating feature when I first gazed upon it. This is a "sweet spot" for safe withdrawal rates for this two-asset portfolio. On the left side of this plateau, corresponding to allocations of less than 35% stocks, SAFEMAX suffered, presumably because bonds lacked the returns required to power withdrawal rates. On the right side of the plateau, at very high stock allocations, a nasty bear market could devastate your portfolio and similarly subdue withdrawal rates. However, the "middle road" of the central plateau saw you safely home under all conditions.

Figure 8.2A illustrates the outcome when there are seven asset classes in the portfolio, not just two, representing my latest research. In

Figure 8.2A   Universal SAFEMAX vs. equity allocation (seven asset classes). Tax-advantaged account, 30 years longevity, January 1 1926–January 1 1993.

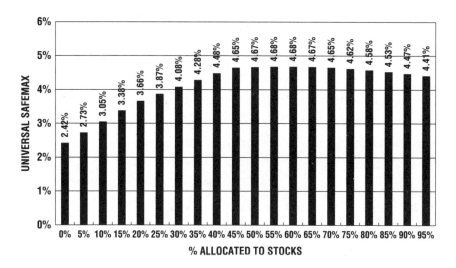

addition to LCS and ITGB, the five new asset classes are US Treasury Bills (TB), US Small-Company Stocks (SCS), US Mid-Cap Stocks (MC), US Micro-Cap Stocks (MIC), and International Stocks (ITS). I assumed that the total stock allocation of the portfolio is evenly distributed among the five stock asset classes mentioned above (we'll revisit this assumption later). Treasury Bills are maintained at a constant 5% allocation throughout.

The most apparent difference between Figures 8.1 and 8.2A is the substantial increase in peak SAFEMAX from about 4.2% to 4.7%. (Does this mean we have a "4.7% rule" now? Heaven forfend!) In this regard, the five additional classes have made a worthwhile improvement! This is a further argument, if one is needed, of the benefits of portfolio diversification. Diversification is the first of four "free lunches" we shall discuss in this book, as it provides higher withdrawal rates without increasing risk.

It's also clear that the additional asset classes have not changed the shapes of the left sides of Figure 8.2A relative to that of Figure 8.1. At lower stock allocations (higher bond allocations), SAFEMAX still drops off steeply. However, there is a significant improvement on the right side in Figure 8.2A, where the penalty for very high stock allocations is far less for the seven-asset portfolio. This results from the favorable interaction among the five stock asset classes. In other words, they have only a modest "correlation" with one another in terms of the timing of their peaks and valleys in performance. Thus, one may adopt higher stock allocations with less concern than before if that is one's preference. Diversification triumphs again.

Figure 8.2B provides a magnified view of the "summit" area of Figure 8.2A. It identifies the absolute peak allocation for Universal SAFEMAX occurring at overall equity allocations between 57% and 62%. *This suggests that if you plan to maintain a static asset allocation during retirement, an allocation to stocks of about 60% is ideal, leaving 35% for bonds and 5% for money market funds (or their equivalent, such as Treasury Bills).*

As a curiosity, the two-asset portfolio from my early research achieved peak Universal SAFEMAX at stock allocations of between 60% and 64%. Thus, adding four stock asset classes reduced the percentage of stocks required to achieve the optimum result. Fewer stocks result in a lower-volatility portfolio with no sacrifice in withdrawal rates. Chalk it up as yet another win for diversification!

As a final observation, it should be noted that ***all*** the withdrawal rates in Figure 8.2B are essentially equivalent, as they differ at most by only 0.04%. Thus, it would not be irrational for investors to choose any of the shown stock allocations. Those preferring a less volatile portfolio would tend toward the left side of the chart while more aggressive investors hoping to build greater wealth would favor the right side.

Figure 8.2B "Summit" Universal SAFEMAX vs. equity allocation (seven asset classes.) Standard configuration, 1 January 1926–1 January 1993.

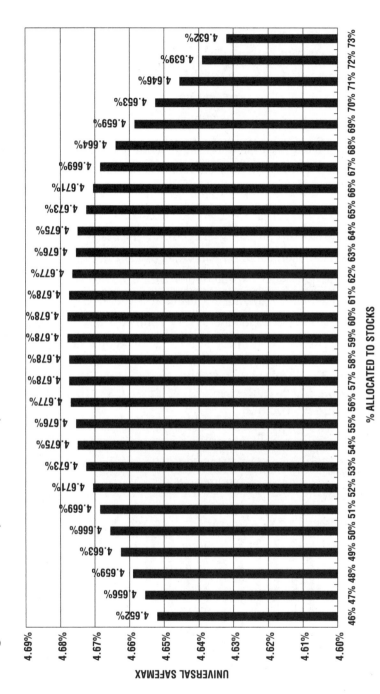

8.3 WHICH ASSET ALLOCATION IS RIGHT FOR ME?

This discussion begs the question, why bother with higher stock alloca-tions? Since SAFEMAX over a wide range of stock allocations is about the same, why not select a stock allocation in the lower range of the summit and enjoy the lower portfolio volatility that comes with it?

To answer this question, let's consider the dollar value of the portfolio after 20 years. Figure 8.3 compares the 20-year value of portfolios with 46% stocks and 73% stocks at the opposite ends of the SAFEMAX "summit." Despite having virtually identical initial withdrawal rates of about 4.7%, the 73% stock portfolio dramatically outperforms its counterpart after 20 years. This is the primary argument for higher stock allocations: the

Figure 8.3 Nominal value of portfolio after 20 years vs. stock allocation. (4.7% IWR) seven asset classes, 5% TB, residue in ITGB, start value = $100,000.

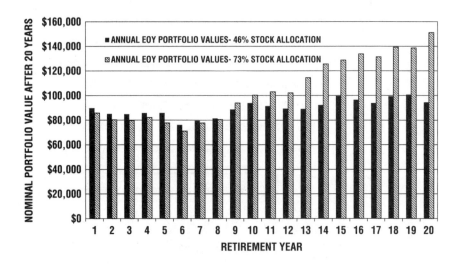

possibility for greater wealth accumulation during retirement is increased, as stocks generally earn much higher returns than bonds.

However, there is a caveat: since both these portfolios, by definition, expire at the end of 30 years, they will both have the same terminal value at the end of that period: zero. Thus, the extra wealth of the 73%-stock portfolio will eventually dissipate. The wealth advantage was only temporary.

Does this invalidate the use of higher stock allocations? Not necessarily. Both of these portfolios were based on "worst-case" scenarios. If actual investment returns are more favorable than anticipated during the last 10 years of retirement, some of that extra wealth may "stick," producing an unexpected legacy. This might not be an unwelcome development!

Now we return to the question, "Which asset allocation is right for me?" From the analysis above, we know that SAFEMAX is about the same over a wide range of stock allocations (46% to 73%). Ultimately, the choice devolves into a trade-off between your own tolerance for volatility and the importance of having a chance for greater wealth later in retirement, perhaps to increase your legacy to heirs. Or maybe star in your own version of "Billions."

For illustration, I often use the "middle ground," or 55% to 60% stocks, as it offers a good balance between volatility and growth of wealth. This choice adheres closely to the traditional "60/40 stock/bond" portfolio you may see often mentioned in the media. Perhaps it will work best for you as well!

8.4   TREASURY BILLS VS. US GOVERNMENT BONDS: WHAT'S THE OPTIMUM MIX?

We now focus on optimizing the asset allocation within our fixed income component (we shall use 45% of all portfolio assets) and our stock component (55%). First, we shall examine our fixed income investments, which consist of only two asset classes: US Treasury Bills and US Government Intermediate-Term Bonds.

The long-term rates of return for both these asset classes appear in Table 8.1. Over the almost 100 years of my primary database, Treasury Bills have enjoyed an average compounded return of 3.2%, and Bonds have returned 4.9%. Given the wide return disparity between the two asset classes, one might expect that Treasury Bills would not justify inclusion as an investment. However, that is not correct for the following reasons:

1. Treasury Bills have virtually zero volatility, meaning their value does not fluctuate. Although bonds are often regarded as "safe" investments, their value can fluctuate significantly, as investors experienced in 2022. As interest rates rose, such bonds lost 6% to 7% of their value for every 1% increase in interest rates. As is frequently experienced in retirement portfolio construction, adding a lower-retuning, lower-volatility asset can improve the overall portfolio's performance.

2. In my analysis, Treasury Bills are a proxy for money market funds and cash. Cash is an essential component of retirement portfolios. Withdrawals must be made from somewhere! Cash also has a psychological benefit, as it allows the investor to "ride out" periods of portfolio decline with equanimity, armed with the knowledge they have enough cash to cover their expenses until their portfolio recovers in value.

3. There have been times in the past – most recently 2009 through 2022 – when Treasury Bills, money market mutual funds, and cash all paid close to zero interest rates. In that environment, investors are virtually forced into riskier investments, such as short-term bonds, longer-term bonds, and even stocks, simply to earn a positive return. The investment environment will affect this fixed income allocation decision.

Table 8.1   Rates of Return for Fixed Income Asset Classes 1926–2022

Fixed Income Asset Class	Compounded Annual Return 1/1/1926 Through 31 December 2022
US Treasury Bills	3.2%
US Govt Int-Term Bonds	4.9%

Having made these points, we turn our attention to Figure 8.4. This chart illustrates the effects on SAFEMAX of varying the fraction of Treasury Bills and Bonds in the portfolio while keeping their total allocation constant. At the left of the chart, Treasury Bills begin at zero allocation and Bonds at 45%. As we move right on the chart, the fraction of Treasury Bills is gradually reduced, and Bonds are concomitantly increased, but their total is always 45% of the portfolio.

Quite frankly, this is a pretty dull chart, but it does contain some instructive points. The most noticeable feature is its shape; as the percentage allocated to Treasury Bills increases (and the percentage dedicated to Bonds declines), SAFEMAX decreases. It does so gradually, linearly: for every 1% increase in Treasury Bills, SAFEMAX decreases about 0.02%.

If maximizing your withdrawals was paramount to you, you might choose to forgo Treasury Bills altogether and invest your entire fixed income allocation in bonds. That would yield an initial withdrawal rate of 7.21%. But that's not very practical, as the portfolio would not have any cash to support withdrawals, and you would have to sell investments continually to fund withdrawals.

As a matter of convenience, I recommend a minimum cash holding of about 5%. This would yield an initial withdrawal rate of 7.11%, only slightly more than 0.1% less than the maximum. It's also equivalent to approximately one year's withdrawals, which might be of some emotional comfort, as one could tolerate an unusually volatile stock market for 12 months without panicking. This amount can easily be bumped up to 6% or 7% without dramatically affecting your withdrawal rate.

Figure 8.4 SAFEMAX vs. fixed income allocation (1 July 1989 retiree). Tax-advantaged account, 30 years longevity, 45% total fixed income/55% stocks.

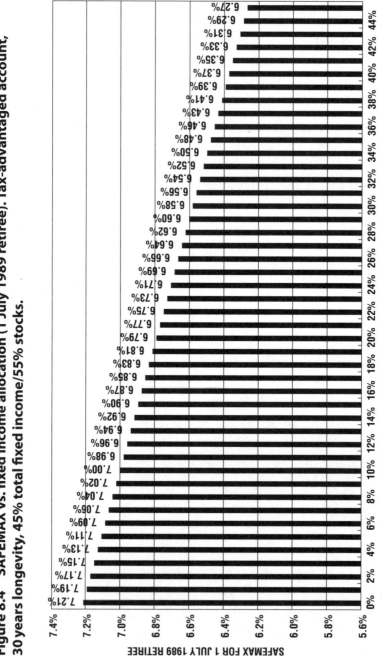

However, large cash holdings, such as 20% or greater, carry a significant penalty. An allocation of 20% in cash decreases the withdrawal rate from 7.11% to 6.79%, or by 4% to 5%. It's hard to justify permanently maintaining a large cash position if one's goal is to withdraw as much as possible. However, under certain threatening market conditions, I consider it perfectly acceptable to temporarily raise cash to that level if the intention is to reduce it to normal levels once the danger has passed. This falls under the "risk management" category and should not threaten the long-term viability of your withdrawal plan. We'll have more to say about risk management in Chapter 13.

8.5 HOW DO I ALLOCATE AMONG MULTIPLE STOCK ASSET CLASSES?

As you recall, my latest research uses five stock asset classes: US Large-Company stocks, US Small-Company stocks, US Mid-cap stocks, US Micro-cap stocks, and International Stocks. Table 8.2 records the long-term (since 1 January 1926) returns earned by each asset class.

Table 8.2 Rates of return for stock asset classes 1926–2022

Stock Asset Class	Compounded Annual Return 1 January 1926 Through 31 December 2022
US Large-Company stocks	10.1%
US Small-Company stocks	11.8%
US Mid-Cap stocks	10.9%
US Micro-Cap stocks	12.0%
International stocks	10.1%

**Figure 8.5   10-year annualized returns for six asset classes
(1 January 1926–1 January 2013)**

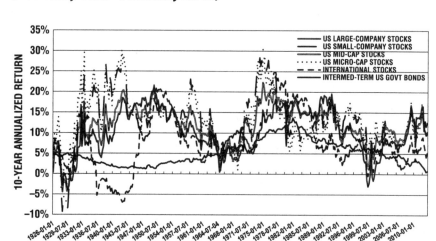

Higher investment returns often produce higher withdrawal rates, so the above table might tempt the unwary investor to place all his assets into only US Small-Company and US Micro-Cap stocks, the two highest-returning stock classes. However, reference to Figure 8.5 suggests that may be an unwise strategy. I apologize in advance for the complexity of this chart, which looks like pasta strips drying on a rack.

This figure compares the 10-year compound annualized return for each of six asset classes (Treasury Bills, which are rather dull, are excluded). I chose the 10-year interval because, as we have learned, what occurs during the first 10–12 years of retirement often significantly impacts withdrawal rates more than what happens later in retirement. It's apparent from the figure that each asset class has been the best performer during certain intervals, and at other intervals, it's been the worst. In other words, every dog has its day.

Let's further explore the practical application of this observation. For example, we know from our prior analysis that an individual retiring on 1

October 1980, had a SAFEMAX of 9.08%. Let's assume that this retiree aggressively alters their stock allocation as follows: LCS 5%, SCS 20%, MCS 5%, MIC 20%, and ITS 5%. In other words, this investor "loads up" their portfolio with the two highest-returning classes and holds minimal holdings in the other three stock classes. How did this retiree fare?

The result is that this investor's SAFEMAX, or safe withdrawal rate, has declined from 9.08% to 8.97%. That's not a huge difference, but the retiree was likely hoping for a significant increase, so this outcome must be very disappointing! The cause of this disaster was timing: as you can see from Figure 8.5, he chose to increase his allocation in two stock classes near their low-performance point. Bad luck!

Equally concerning, however, is that the investor has concentrated his portfolio in the two most volatile stock asset classes. This makes the entire portfolio more volatile and psychologically makes it harder for the individual to "hang in there" when the going gets rough in stocks with a "buy-and-hold" strategy if that is their intention. Investment decisions driven by fear are usually bad decisions.

The conclusion I have drawn from examining many other similar examples is that it's best to distribute your allocation among all stock classes equally. It's almost impossible to predict which stock asset classes will do best in the future and which will do less well, so why try? However, as we shall see below, it can be beneficial to *slightly* overweight the two highest-returning classes.

8.6 EVEN MORE ASSET CLASSES?

Would adding even more asset classes to the portfolio significantly increase SAFEMAX? After all, many other options are available, such as commodities, precious metals, real estate, international small and mid-cap stocks, emerging market bonds, bitcoin, junk bonds, long-term US Treasury bonds, alternative investments, etc.

Adding a few more asset classes would likely, in fact, increase Universal SAFEMAX for our standard configuration from 4.7% to something higher. However, I question whether that increase would be very significant. As you may recall, in 2021, I increased the number of asset classes included in my analysis from three to seven, and SAFEMAX rose from about 4.5% to only about 4.7%. That's pretty minimal! I suspect we are now in the realm of diminishing returns, and further additions might not succeed in pushing SAFEMAX as high as 5.0%. Stay tuned, though, as I plan to keep trying!

8.7 EXOTICA: ALICE IN ASSETLAND

Let's take a journey down the rabbit hole and explore some of the more exotic issues relating to asset allocation. First, let's take a closer look at Figure 8.5. This chart, as you recall, depicts the annualized returns for six of my current asset classes over the first 10 years of each retirement date, 1 January 1926 through 1 January 2013. US Treasury Bills, which are not used as diversifiers but primarily as a proxy for a source of ready cash, are excluded.

To understand the chart better, let's follow one of the asset classes, International Stocks (ITS), across history, beginning at the far left. In the 1920s and early 1930s, ITS was consistently one of the best-performing classes. Then, starting in the middle 1930s and extending through the 1940s, its performance began to lag against all other assets, even bonds. It consistently generated negative 10-year returns. This was presumably connected with World War II.

By the early 1950s, however, ITS had regained its position of preeminence, which it maintained for a few short years till the mid-1950s. Then it began a decade-long period of underperformance. It strengthened again into the late 1960s, then became a middling performer in the 1970s. It resumed its leadership position in the late 1970s and early 1980s. From the late 1980s, ITS remained at or near the bottom of all five stock classes, and from the right end of the chart, there was a 30-year period of underperformance.

This roller-coaster ride is representative of just about every stock asset class. Bonds (as you can see from the line representing US Government Intermediate-Term Bonds) behave somewhat differently; they are less volatile and more likely to produce consistent (if lower) returns. However, they can be affected by long-term ("secular") bull and bear markets, which have spanned decades. This is evident from studying the line for Intermediate-Term US Government Bonds in the figure.

Next, let's follow the White Rabbit down the hole a bit further and conduct a bold experiment to place the lessons of Figure 8.5 into sharper focus. Till now, we have frequently used our standard configuration asset allocation of 5% US Treasury Bills, 40% Intermediate-Term US Government Bonds, and 55% of the portfolio equally weighted among five stock asset classes. What if we retained only the constant 5% US Treasury Bills requirement and allowed the remaining allocation to shift unconstrained, aiming to achieve the highest SAFEMAX for each retiree?

Figure 8.6 shows the results of this optimization process. (In color, this chart makes great wallpaper!) I have elected to end the chart with the 1 January 1993 retiree to assure at least 30 years of actual investment data for each retiree; this is the "stalwart" group I referred to earlier. I have split Figure 8.6 into two charts (Figures 8.6A and 8.6B) to make it easier to view the results. With almost 270 retirees, that was essential!

Figure 8.6A Optimal asset allocation for individual SAFEMAX 1 January 1926–I October 1959

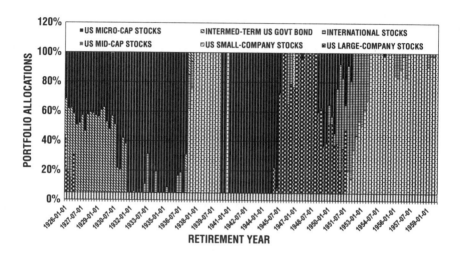

Figure 8.6B Optimal asset allocation for individual SAFEMAX 1 January 1960–1 January 1993

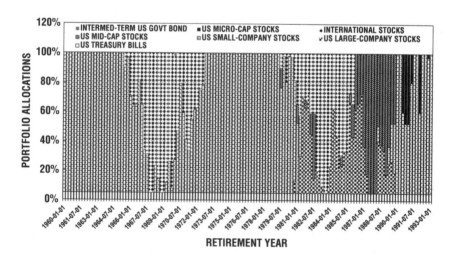

Each column in Figures 8.6A and 8.6B represents the fixed asset allocation of a retiree, which produced the highest safe withdrawal rate for that retiree for 30 years. Within each column, each asset class is represented by a bar identified with a unique pattern, and the height of each bar matches the percentage that the asset represents of the total portfolio. Thank you for looking at this chart, as it took me almost a month to develop the data for it! Here are some trenchant observations:

1. Over time, different asset classes dominate the portfolios. In many cases, only one asset class (other than the invariant 5% allocation to US Treasury Bills) comprises the entire portfolio.

2. There is a close correlation between Figure 8.5 and Figures 8.6A and 8.6B. Asset classes with dominant 10-year returns in Figure 8.5 usually dominate the asset allocation of the corresponding retiree in Figures 8.6A and 8.6B.

3. Rarely do more than two asset classes (aside from US Treasury Bills) appear in the same retirement year allocation.

4. Bonds contribute virtually nothing to allocation after the early 1930s. Perhaps this is not surprising, given their low returns compared to stocks. However, this contrasts dramatically with our standard allocation of 40% to bonds.

5. Overall, the two most dominant asset classes are US Small-Company Stocks and US Micro-Cap Stocks. Again, this is perhaps not surprising, as they are the asset classes with the two highest long-term returns.

I hope you agree that Figures 8.6A and 8.6B are extraordinary. By themselves, they make our journey to AssetLand worthwhile! They indicate that the optimal allocation is almost never the 55%/45% standard we have considered in earlier discussions and that more than two stock asset classes are rarely required to secure the optimum result.

Table 8.3 lists the average unconstrained allocation for each asset class across all retirement dates. US Small-Company Stocks and US Micro-Cap Stocks dominated; together, they accounted for over 60% of the average unconstrained allocation. The average allocation is 91.2% stocks and 8.8% fixed income. That's a long way from our standard 55%/45% portfolio, which now appears to be a bit of a Cheshire Cat, grinning at us mischievously!

Table 8.3   Average unconstrained asset allocation

Asset Class	Average Allocation
US Large-Company stocks	10.20%
US Small-Company stocks	41.75%
US Mid-Size-Company stocks	4.33%
US Micro-Cap stocks	20.95%
International stocks	14.00%
Intermediate-Term US Govt Bonds	3.77%
US Treasury Bills (FORCED)	5.00%
Total	100.00%

Before we consider the ramifications of these observations, examine Figure 8.7A, which depicts the individual SAFEMAX values generated by the unconstrained allocation and compares it to the SAFEMAX for our "standard" allocation. *As you can see, the unconstrained SAFEMAX is higher for every retiree.* The difference is quite considerable: an average SAFEMAX of 11.72% for unconstrained vs. an average of 7.25% for standard. This represents an increase of 59% in SAFEMAX!

Two other features of Figure 8.7A are worth noting. The peak SAFEMAX for the unconstrained allocation is an astounding 49.5%, more than triple that of the standard allocation. It was achieved with an allocation of 95% in

Figure 8.7A   Individual SAFEMAX for "equal-weighted stocks" and "unconstrained" allocations. Tax-advantaged account, 30 years longevity, 5% US Treasury Bills, remainder of allocation as specified.

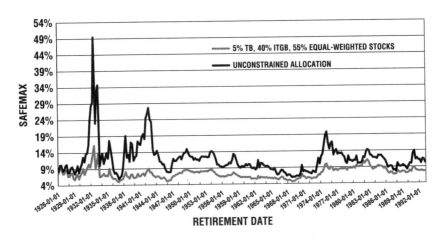

Micro-Cap stocks. Imagine withdrawing at a 50% rate during retirement! The lucky individual was the 1 July 1932 retiree, who managed to retire almost precisely at the bottom of the 90% stock decline of 1929–1932. Great timing!

Furthermore, the worst-case Universal SAFEMAX, achieved by the 1 October 1968 retiree, was 6.0% for the unconstrained allocation vs. our previous determination of 4.7% for the standard allocation.

Does this mean we can now discuss "the 6% rule"?

Unfortunately, it's not that easy. Being a retiree myself, I wish it were. The White Rabbit has led us on a bit of a wild-goose chase.

The fly in the ointment is that, to the best of my knowledge, we can't predict the optimum asset allocation for any retiree. It's as difficult a proposition as "market timing": selling equities at a major market top and repurchasing them at almost precisely the succeeding market bottom. I don't know of anyone who has succeeded in doing so on a consistent, long-term basis. Some have gone broke trying.

Plus, the stakes are much more significant here. If a retiree mistimes the market, they may get another chance to get it right in five to seven years. However, if a retiree fails in their choice of initial asset allocation, they may have killed their retirement. That's because the asset allocation decision is for 30 years, not five to seven. As with most other things in the depths of the rabbit hole, unconstrained allocation is thus largely an illusion.

Still, the allure of such stellar withdrawal rates is nigh irresistible. Isn't there a way we can adjust our approach to enjoy a seat next to the Mad Hatter at the Tea Party? Could we, for example, increase SAFEMAX by adopting an allocation that slightly favors the best-performing asset classes, namely US Micro-Cap and US Small-Company Stocks, but still appears reasonably balanced? For example, what if we changed the allocation as indicated in Table 8.4?

Table 8.4   Suggested change to asset allocation

Asset Class	Standard Allocation	Test Allocation
US Large-Company stocks	11%	15%
US Small-Company stocks	11%	15%
US Mid-Size-Company stocks	11%	11%
US Micro-Cap stocks	11%	11%
International stocks	11%	11%
Intermediate-term US Govt Bonds	40%	32%
US Treasury Bills	5%	5%
Total	100%	100%

The "test allocation" reduces the percentage of low-returning bonds in exchange for an increased fraction of higher-returning stock classes. Overall, the portfolio is converted from a 55%/45% stock/fixed income allocation to 63%/37%. It's a modest change overall, but in retirement investing, small input differences can lead to large changes in outcomes.

Figure 8.7B   Individual SAFEMAX for "equal-weighted stocks" and "test" allocations. Tax-advantaged account, 30 years longevity, 5% US Treasury Bills, remainder of allocation as specified.

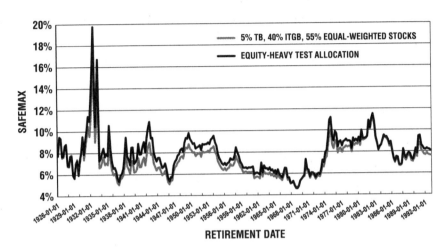

To evaluate the effectiveness of this change, I re-computed the individual SAFEMAX for each of 269 "stalwart" retirees (retiring from 1 January 1926 through 1 January 1993), using the test allocation. The results are depicted in Figure 8.7B and are compared to the earlier computations for the "equal-weighted-stocks" allocation.

As you can see, in the vast majority of cases (95%), the test portfolio produces a higher SAFEMAX; in many cases, it is much higher. The average SAFEMAX for the test allocation is 7.9%, vs. about 7.4% for the "equal-weighted-stock" allocation, an increase of about 7%. Would you like to have 7% more to spend yearly in retirement? Don't answer; that's a rhetorical question!

There are limited periods where the test allocation is inferior or offers only a modest improvement in SAFEMAX. Unfavorable comparisons include the late 1920s (just preceding the massive stock bear market of the early 1930s) and around the "worst-case" scenario of the late 1960s (back-to-back bear markets and high inflation). However, none of the negative comparisons are as bad as −3%, with the average dip less than −1.5%. In the early 1980s, there was little to choose between the two allocations, as their SAFEMAX were virtually identical.

My last concern was the effect of the new allocation on the "Universal" SAFEMAX or "worst-case" scenario. Adopting the test allocation shifted the date of the worst-case scenario from 1 October 1968 to an adjacent retirement date, 1 January 1969. The value of Universal SAFEMAX declined in the process from 4.676% to 4.600%, only about a 1.5% reduction.

Summing up: the test allocation affords a higher SAFEMAX in the vast majority of cases while the rest suffer a mild degradation, including the Universal SAFEMAX. I would say that this approach looks extremely promising, as it offers the prospect of significantly higher withdrawal rates to a large percentage of retirees. In my mind, this represents another "free lunch" for investors.

I have a few minor concerns about this approach, though. For one, increasing a portfolio's concentration in small-company and micro-cap stocks will notably increase its volatility, which might be upsetting to the investor. Furthermore, if many people were to adopt the test allocation, it would significantly increase the demand for smaller company stocks, which are never in great supply. That might adversely affect the prices of those stocks and eliminate their historical edge in investment returns.

Still, those are minor objections, and I wouldn't shrink from this approach for those reasons. For consistency, where applicable, I will continue to use the "standard" allocation for the rest of this book. Overall, however, I rate our journey down the rabbit hole a success. It's made us aware of some intriguing possibilities that additional research might further enhance. However, it's time to consume the "Eat Me" cake and return to the everyday world to study relatively mundane but very important asset allocation issues.

8.8 OPTIMUM ASSET ALLOCATION VS. PLANNING HORIZON

Will all retirees benefit from the same "standard" asset allocation regardless of planning horizon? This question is partially addressed in Figure 8.8, which depicts the asset allocation for SAFEMAX for various retirement planning horizons. Note that this chart applies only to the "worst-case" retiree, who retired on 31 October 1968.

Figure 8.8 Optimum stock allocation vs. planning horizon (1 October 1968 retiree). Tax-advantaged account, seven asset classes, equal-weighted stocks, allocation corresponding to SAFEMAX.

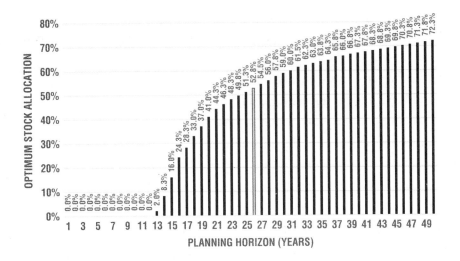

Figure 8.9 Optimum stock allocation vs. retirement time horizon (1 July 1989 retiree). Tax-advantaged account, seven asset classes, equal-weighted stocks, allocation corresponding to SAFEMAX.

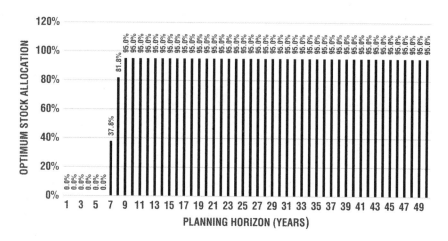

As per the chart, for very short planning horizons, the highest withdrawal rate is achieved by not using any stocks at all; the ideal allocation consisted of only Intermediate-Term US Government Bonds and US Treasury Bills. As the planning horizon lengthens, stocks become increasingly important. At the 30-year mark, the ideal allocation of stocks was 59% for this retiree, and the optimum stock allocation continues to increase with the planning horizon.

However, assuming that the above observations apply to all retirees would be a mistake. Figure 8.9 examines optimum horizon-dependent allocations for the 1 July 1989 retiree, whom we have used as an example earlier. This is a dramatically different-appearing chart from Figure 8.8, as stock allocations rise rapidly and early and almost fill the portfolio by year nine!

The situation is even more extreme in Figure 8.10, which reflects the experience of the 1 January 1975 retiree. Stock allocations are maxed out from the "git-go" beginning in year one. There is no hint of any need for any bonds, for any planning horizon.

Figure 8.10   Optimum stock allocation vs. retirement time horizon (1 January 1975). Tax-advantaged account, seven asset classes, equal-weighted stocks, allocation corresponding to SAFEMAX.

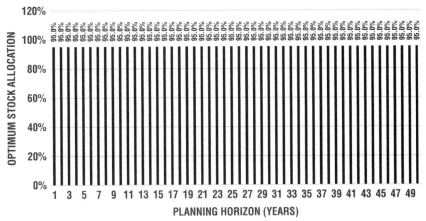

Why such disparate experiences for these three retirees? And what does it teach us about allocating portfolios based on planning horizon?

The disparities' root cause is the phenomenon that underlies overall variation in SAFEMAX. All other factors being equal, the earlier an investor experiences a substantial bear market in retirement, the greater the reduction of their withdrawal rates. In this case, the equivalent phenomenon is that early bear markets lead to more conservative allocations, particularly for short planning horizons.

Let's consider each of our three sample retirees individually. The 1 October 1968 retiree experienced two major bear markets early in retirement (1969–1970 and 1973–1974) and high inflation during the first half of retirement. Thus, it makes sense that their allocation for short planning horizons would contain few, if any, stocks, as otherwise the withdrawal rate would be diminished by losses in stocks. By way of reference, the compounded annual portfolio return for this retiree for the first five years (using a standard "equal-stock-weight" allocation) was a measly 7.0% (vs. an average of 10% for all the retirees in my database).

By contrast, the 1 July 1989 retiree enjoyed quitting work in the middle of a huge secular bull market (1982–2000) with only a minor, short bear market (related to the first Gulf War) experienced in their first year of retirement. This retiree's compounded annual portfolio return for the first five years was a healthier (but still below average) 8.9%. These factors contributed to a higher tolerance for stocks in early retirement years.

Finally, the individual who retired on 1 January 1975 did so just days after the nasty 1973–1974 bear market ended. Despite a period of high inflation, subsequent very high stock market returns supported high withdrawal rates, as no bear market was encountered over the first seven years. This retiree's compounded annual portfolio return for the first five years was an astonishing 18.7%.

I've examined many other retirement scenarios in this light, and the results vary significantly from one retiree to another, as with our three examples above. *Therefore, I have concluded that there is no specific advice that can be given as to the optimum allocation for a portfolio of a given planning horizon.* Historically, there has been a very wide range of outcomes.

However, as alluded to above, allocation outcomes are heavily influenced by "initial conditions," which means the likelihood of a stock bear market in the early retirement years. This observation may provide a useful, if perhaps subjective, means of estimating best allocations for various planning horizons.

For example, the 1 October 1968 retiree could be cited as an example of "high bear market risk"; the 1 July 1989 retiree as an example of "moderate risk"; and the 1 January 1975 retiree as "low risk." Their respective asset allocation/planning horizon charts could be used as paradigms for each class of risk. This is a relatively crude approach, but it would appear to get the direction correct.

In most cases, market valuation is a fair indicator of bear market risk, although the lag until the onset of the bear market is uncertain. The more expensive the market, the higher the risk. Bear markets rarely occur when the stock market is cheap (1980–1982 being an exception, owing to Volcker's actions to contain inflation) and are more likely to happen when markets are expensive (e.g., 1929, 1937, 1966, 2000, 2007, and 2022).

If you prefer not to deal with all this complexity and uncertainty, Figure 8.8, for the 1 October 1968 retiree, can be used as an "all seasons" allocation that has worked under the direst of past circumstances. For those especially averse to risk, it is a helpful guide.

8.9   VARYING EQUITY ALLOCATION DURING RETIREMENT: IS IT EFFECTIVE?

Until now, we have specified that the same portfolio allocation should be maintained during retirement, with annual portfolio rebalancing keeping us firmly "on target." However, is that assumption justified? It's time to scrutinize this assumption, as we should ultimately do with all our underlying assumptions.

At the outset, I would like to mention that other researchers have studied this issue, and I have benefited from their insights. Their works are listed in Appendix B. Some, (notably Wade Pfau and Michael Kitces, two of the luminaries in financial research), have used the term "rising glidepath" to describe a continuous, gradual increase in equity allocation during retirement. I will borrow that terminology with a proper show of respect.

Early in my research, I studied declining asset allocation during retirement and concluded that it was counterproductive. To illustrate that, let's consider the effect of *decreasing* glidepath allocation on the three retirees we discussed in the last section, each representing a different investment retirement early in retirement: 1 October 1968, 1 January 1975, and 1 October 1989.

Figure 8.11 shows, for each of these three investors, the effect on SAFEMAX of increasing or decreasing overall equity allocation each successive year by a fixed amount. The exact middle of the chart, at 0% glidepath, is our "standard" fixed allocation, which we have used in almost all our discussions up to this point. To the left are declining glidepaths of various magnitudes, and to the right are rising glidepaths. A "−0/2% glidepath" means that the overall stock allocation is reduced by 0.2% each year. Within the overall stock allocation, each of the five asset classes is reduced annually by an equal percentage. I limit the glidepath to a maximum of 30 years, so a −0.2% glidepath will reduce stocks overall by 6% at the end of that time period. If the initial stock allocation is 55%, stocks will have been reduced to 49% after 30 years, but their allocation will remain unchanged after that.

Figure 8.11 Individual SAFEMAX for "glidepath" allocations – three retirees. Tax-advantaged account, 5% US Treasury Bills, 30 years longevity begin with 55% equal-weighted stocks, change stocks proportionately.

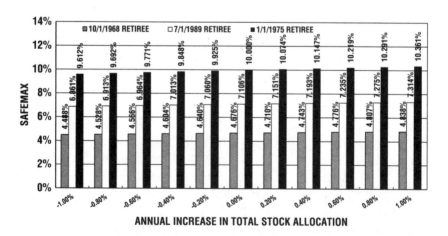

ANNUAL INCREASE IN TOTAL STOCK ALLOCATION

Let's first study the left side of Figure 8.11, which depicts declining stock allocations. SAFEMAX declines when we reduce stock allocations during retirement. Furthermore, the steeper the declining glidepath, the lower the SAFEMAX. This observation supports my conclusions from 1996: a declining glidepath deleteriously affects retirement withdrawal rates.

However, I never bothered to look at rising glidepaths, represented on the right side of Figure 8.11, until research on the topic was published. Why not? Quite frankly, I had a blind spot. I recalled the conclusions of charts like Figure 8.2A, which shows that when using fixed allocations, there is an optimum range for stock allocations, and if you exceed that, it reduces SAFEMAX. I overlooked utterly the possibility that the dynamics of a continually increasing stock allocation were completely different from those of a static allocation, so I never bothered to explore the possibilities on my own. Shame on me!

Examining the right side of Figure 8.11 does confirm the finding of Pfau and Kitces (and others) that a rising glidepath allocation during retirement increases SAFEMAX, with little or no risk. Chalk up another free lunch for retiree investors!

Note that each of our three sample retirees experienced a significant increase in SAFEMAX using a rising glidepath. Furthermore, the steeper the glidepath (meaning the more rapid the rise in stock allocation), the higher the SAFEMAX! Note also that for the rightmost group of bars, corresponding to a 1% rising glidepath, the stock allocation in year 30 of retirement will be 85%, much higher than recommended when using fixed allocations.

Figure 8.12 compares the effect on SAFEMAX of a 1% rising equity glidepath vs. a fixed equity allocation, for all "stalwart" retirees (those retiring 1 January 1926–1 January 1993). As you can see, for all 269 retirees, the 1% glidepath produces a higher SAFEMAX for every retiree, without exception. This is an extraordinary result and serves to underline the usefulness of the rising glidepath concept.

Figure 8.12   SAFEMAX for "fixed" and "1% rising glidepath" allocations (1 January 1926–1 January 1993). Tax-advantaged account, 30 years longevity 5% US Treasury Bills, remainder of allocation as specified.

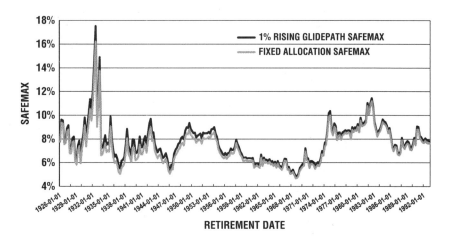

Figure 8.13 casts a microscope on Figure 8.12, focusing on the percentage difference between the rising glidepath and the fixed equity allocation. Not all retirees benefit equally, as you can see. The rising glidepath improved on the fixed allocation by between 2% and 10%, with the average for all retirees being about 5%. This is certainly a worthwhile increase in retirement income!

The "glory years" for rising glidepath were 1 July 1929 through 1 October 1949, when glidepath SAFEMAX consistently exceeded fixed allocation SAFEMAX by at least 6%. Most recently, in the 1980s and 1990s, during the great bull market, gains have been far more modest but still worthwhile.

Under a rising glidepath, the Universal SAFEMAX for our standard configuration (the 1 October 1968 retiree) is increased from 4.68% to 4.84%. Does this mean we now have a "4.8% rule" instead of a "4.7% rule"? Apparently so, but excuse me, I'm not going there!

Figure 8.13   Percentage difference in SAFEMAX for "fixed" and "1% increasing glidepath" allocations. Tax-advantaged account, 30 years longevity, 5% US Treasury Bills, 1 January 1926– l1 January 1993.

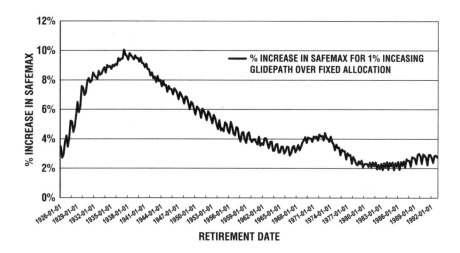

Perhaps you noted the odd "saw-toothed" pattern of Figure 8.13. In fact, I nickname this chart "Jaws." The odd shape is attributable to the fact that SAFEMAX for both fixed and glidepath allocations has always risen and fallen simultaneously (although by differing amounts), creating the peculiar look.

Of course, all this begs the question, why do glidepaths work? Why don't such high stock allocations later in retirement cause the portfolio to blow up? Instead, they are even more productive in generating sustainable withdrawals than are fixed asset allocations.

In their 2013 paper, Pfau and Kitces offer the following explanation: ". . . in a situation where the first half of retirement is bad (e.g., the 1929 or late 1960s retiree), rising equity exposure leads the retiree to systematically dollar cost average into equities through flat or declining markets, maximizing exposure by the time the good returns finally show up (e.g., after

World War II or starting in the 1980s) and helping to sustain greater retirement income over the entire time period." In other words, in the scenarios where equity returns are bad early on, rising equity glidepaths are crucial, and in scenarios where equity returns are good early on, the retiree is so far ahead it doesn't matter (relative to achieving the original goal). I concur with their conclusions.

Pfau and Kitces concluded in their 2013 paper that best results were achieved with the rising glidepath method by using lower initial equity allocations than the 55% I employed in Figures 8.12 and 8.13. Thus, even larger increases in SAFEMAX may be achievable than I have illustrated here.

In sum, I consider the rising glidepath method a big success and recommend it for your consideration. Although I will continue to use the fixed allocation method in the remainder of this book for the sake of simplicity, keep in the back of your mind you can enhance all SAFEMAX figures by using "rising glidepath."

In the next chapter, we examine how SAFEMAX is affected by changing the planning horizon from our "standard" of 30 years.

CHAPTER 9

ELEMENT #6: PORTFOLIO REBALANCING

"Portfolio rebalancing" means periodically returning the portfolio to its original asset allocation by selling investments that have exceeded their original allocation and buying investments that have fallen below their original allocation. This process intends to prevent the portfolio from deviating too wildly from its original intended level of risk.

Portfolios may be rebalanced in several ways. One variation is to rebalance all assets in the portfolio simultaneously and return the entire portfolio to its original allocation, wholesale. Another variation is establishing "guardrails" for each asset, tracking their performance over time, and rebalancing only assets that have strayed outside their tolerance levels. There are other possibilities as well.

How frequently should you rebalance your portfolio? In my 2006 book, I examined this question and concluded that SAFEMAX increased significantly (about 5%) by increasing the "rebalancing interval" (the time between rebalancing events) from 12 months to 75 months. However, rebalancing at even longer intervals was unproductive as SAFEMAX declined. At very long rebalancing intervals, SAFEMAX fell below its value for 12-month rebalancing.

In this book, I will re-examine the topic in greater detail. Given that I now work with seven asset classes, not three, as I did during the preparation of my 2006 book, let's not be surprised if my earlier conclusions require alteration.

9.1 SAFEMAX VS. PORTFOLIO REBALANCING INTERVAL

To explore this topic in a relevant manner, I selected 20 retirees from the 269 "stalwarts" (that have 30 full years of historical data). I chose the earliest retiree (1 January 1926), the latest retiree (1 January 1993), and a group of evenly spaced retirees between those dates. Granted, this is not an authentic random sample, but it does have the merit of representing all historical periods. I tested how SAFEMAX varied for each retiree as I changed the "rebalancing interval."

I chose to test rebalancing at the end of calendar quarters; e.g., portfolios were rebalanced at the end of one quarter, at the end of two quarters, and so on, up to a maximum of 20 quarters (five years). All testing was done with "standard configuration" portfolios, i.e., beginning with 55% stocks, 40% bonds and 5% cash, with all five stock asset classes equally weighted.

Figure 9.1   SAFEMAX vs. rebalancing interval (20-retiree average). Tax-advantaged account, 30 years longevity, seven asset classes, 55%/40%/5% stocks/bonds/cash.

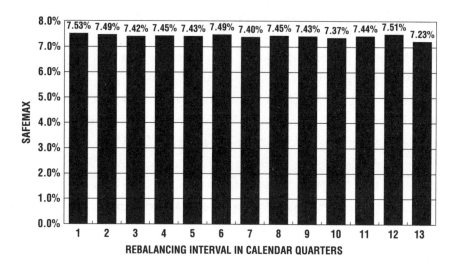

I also tested rebalancing at the end of the 121st quarter; this is tantamount to not rebalancing at all, since this is beyond the 30-year planning horizon. Unlike earlier testing, I specified that all income and capital gains dividends be reinvested in their source funds and not paid in cash to the Treasury Bill asset class. I did this so that each asset class could grow at its own compounded rate, driven by its historical rate of return.

Figure 9.1 shows the outcome of our experiment. At first blush, this chart appears rather dull, but I assure you it contains valuable nuggets of information. The shortest rebalancing period, one quarter, appears at the left of the chart, with the length of the rebalancing interval increasing as we move right on the chart. The rightmost bar represents a rebalancing interval of 121 months, which, as mentioned earlier, is effectively "no rebalancing" for a 30-year planning horizon.

Let's focus first on rebalancing intervals from 1 to 12 quarters. The height of each bar represents the average SAFEMAX of the 20 test portfolios at the indicated rebalancing interval. The variation in SAFEMAX across all intervals is quite tiny; approximately 2% separates the highest SAFEMAX (7.53%) from the lowest SAFEMAX (7.37%). Statistically, all the SAFEMAX are virtually equal. There does not appear to be an identifiable trend in the chart.

The apparent conclusion from a cursory examination of Figure 9.1 is that the length of the rebalancing interval makes little difference to the retiree, as all seem to produce about the same SAFEMAX. What is clear is that not rebalancing can be harmful, as the lowest SAFEMAX value is attributed to the 121-quarter bar. However, this chart is an average for 20 retirees, and assuming that all retirees had a similar experience would be dangerous. After all, we don't want to be the six-foot person who drowned in a lake with an average depth of four feet!

In fact, there were significant differences in the experience of individual retirees. Let's examine charts for two retirees with more extreme experiences to illuminate these differences further. Figure 9.2 provides a detailed look at the SAFEMAX-vs.-rebalancing interval for the 1 July 1927 retiree. Clearly, this chart is "a whole'nother smoke" from the previous one. There is quite a bit of volatility in SAFEMAX, especially through the 23-quarter interval, after which it effectively subsides.

You many notice the steep drop in SAFEMAX from the 20th to the 21st quarter – almost three full percentage points! At first blush, such an outcome doesn't even seem possible; what circumstances could cause this astounding result? The answer is after more than three years of decline at the beginning of the Great Depression, stocks finally bottomed at the end of the 20th quarter (June 1932). If you rebalanced at the end of that quarter (which was a terrible quarter for stocks, with 30% to 40% losses), your portfolio would have gotten the full benefit of the enormous 100%+ gains of the following quarter (you read that correctly – many stock classes more

Figure 9.2   SAFEMAX vs. rebalancing interval (1 July 1927 retiree). Tax-advantaged account, 30 years longevity, seven asset classes, 50%/40%/5% stocks/bonds/cash.

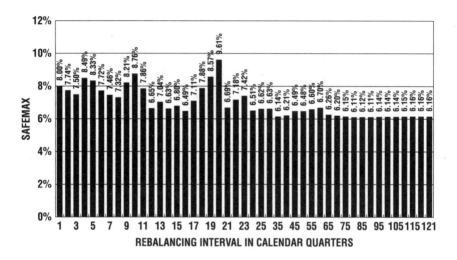

than doubled in just three months). If you didn't rebalance and waited just one quarter, you would have lost out on the full effect of those gains, and your withdrawal rate would have been savaged.

I am no longer a buy-and-hold investor (I believe in a risk management approach, explained later in this book), but I have probably just handed the buy-and-hold crowd the biggest weapon in their arsenal. Staying in the market, fully invested, was the right thing to do in June 1932. But it was hard to do after suffering almost 90% losses the prior three-and-a-half years. Investing is never easy!

Let's look at one more retiree before moving on to general conclusions about rebalancing intervals. Figure 9.3 provides comparable data for the 1 July 1941 retiree. This chart paints an entirely different picture than the two preceding charts. It shows a clear rising trend of SAFEMAX with increasing rebalancing interval; the longer one delayed rebalancing, the higher the SAFEMAX. There are no very steep "cliffs" as there were in Figure 9.2 between the 20-quarter and 21-quarter intervals.

Figure 9.3 SAFEMAX vs. rebalancing interval (1 July 1941 retiree). Tax-advantaged account, seven asset classes, 55%/40%/5% stocks/bonds/cash.

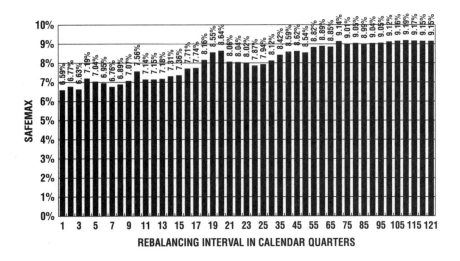

We've examined a lot of data together. What can we conclude about balancing frequency? I suggest the following:

1. Although, *on average*, rebalancing makes little difference to the SAFEMAX of retirees, it may play a large role for certain individual retirees.

2. Generally, retirees who experience a large bear market early in their retirement (such as the 1 July 1927 retiree) are better off deferring rebalancing (i.e., taking longer intervals between rebalancing).

3. Retirees who do not encounter a large bear market early in their retirement (such as the 1 July 1941 retiree) improve their SAFEMAX by more frequent rebalancing.

4. Rebalancing every fourth quarter (i.e., at the end of every investment year) produced a decent SAFEMAX for virtually all historical

retirees and represents a reasonable compromise. Judging accurately whether a bear market is close or far away is not always possible, so this compromise is practical.

5. The choice of rebalancing interval is not permanent and may be altered during retirement to take advantage of changing conditions.

These conclusions are at odds with conclusions I reached in my 2006 book. That's a product of several factors, including working with more asset classes and taking a more comprehensive look at the issue (e.g., not focusing on just the 31 October 1968 retiree as I did in 2006).

9.2 PORTFOLIO REBALANCING VS. GLIDEPATH INVESTING

At the end of 30 years, assuming 121-quarter rebalancing (effectively, no rebalancing) the average overall allocation for the 20 retirees was 87% stocks and 13% bonds. Thus, having begun at a stock allocation of 55%, stock allocations increased by approximately 1% per year for the average retiree. There was considerable variation in this statistic among retirees, ranging from a low of 74% stocks to a high of 98% stocks.

In our earlier discussion of "rising glidepath investing," we successfully tested increasing overall equity allocation by 1% per year, which is very similar to the above outcome. This begs the question: Is declining to rebalance as effective a strategy in raising SAFEMAX as rising glidepath investing?

The short answer to this is a resounding "No!" If you recall, using rising glidepath investing, all retirees experienced an increase in SAFEMAX, although the magnitude of the benefit varied from retiree to retiree. That is not the case for "zero rebalancing"; it caused most of the

20 test retirees to have a lower SAFEMAX. This outcome is due to the unevenness of the increase in equity allocation; in some years, equity allocations decreased for some retirees. Thus, zero rebalancing is no substitute for glidepath investing. Even if it ends up in the same place allocation-wise, the journey is less productive for SAFEMAX.

9.3   REBALANCING AND PORTFOLIO RETURNS

Based on the historical rates of return for its component asset classes, what overall rate of return should we expect from our retirement portfolio? Table 9.1 computes this.

Table 9.1   Expected portfolio rate of return computation

Asset Class	Annual Rate of Return 1926–2022	Starting Allocation	Contribution to Return
US Large-Company stocks	10.1%	11%	1.11%
US Small-Company stocks	11.8%	11%	1.30%
US Mid-Size-Company stocks	10.9%	11%	1.20%
US Micro-Cap stocks	12.0%	11%	1.32%
International stocks	10.1%	11%	1.11%
US Treasury Bills	3.2%	5%	0.16%
US Intermediate-Term Govt Bonds	4.9%	40%	1.96%
One-year projected average rate of return			8.16%

Figure 9.4   Cumulative portfolio rates of return 1 January 1926 retiree (4-quarter and no rebalancing). Tax-advantaged account, 30 years longevity, seven asset classes, initial 55%/40%/5% stocks/bonds/cash.

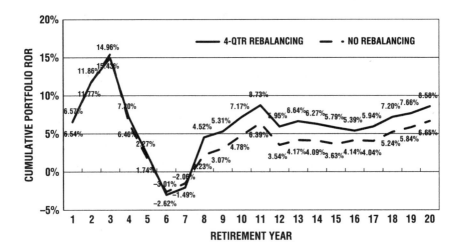

Although the expected average annual return of our starting portfolio is about 8.2%, the average compounded annual return for the portfolios of all our retirees is much higher, about 10%. What is the source of this disparity?

To answer this question, consider Figure 9.4, which shows the annualized rate of return for the portfolio of the 1 January 1926 retiree for the first 20 years of retirement. The results are displayed for two different balancing intervals: rebalancing every four quarters and rebalancing every 121 quarters, which effectively does not rebalance at all over a 20-year planning horizon.

The rates of return are very similar for both intervals through year six, after which they begin to diverge. Over the last 13 years, the rebalanced portfolio enjoyed a significantly higher rate of return, almost two full percentage points above that of the non-rebalanced portfolio. This outcome is very similar to the 2-point advantage in portfolio return all retirees have experienced vs. our tabular computation above.

The only difference between these two portfolios is that one is rebalanced periodically, and one is not. ***Thus, rebalancing is the only explanation for the difference in investment performance.*** We may conclude, therefore, that rebalancing can significantly increase the rate of return of a portfolio. Potentially, this could lead to higher withdrawal rates, although the correlation between portfolio returns and SAFEMAX is surprisingly weak (see Figure 9.5).

We know from our earlier discussion that this is not always the case: for some retirees, not rebalancing leads to higher withdrawal rates. But these situations are in the minority. The key to the success of rebalancing is the timing of the rebalancing vs. the occurrence of a major stock bear market. For the 1 January 1926 investor year seven (1932) marked the bottom of the massive bear market of the Great Depression. Rebalancing primed the portfolio to take advantage of the subsequent market recovery.

Figure 9.5   SAFEMAX vs. 30-year portfolio rate of return (259 retirees 1 January 1926–1 January 1993). Tax-advantaged account, 30 years longevity, seven asset classes, fixed 55%/40%/5% stocks/ bonds/cash.

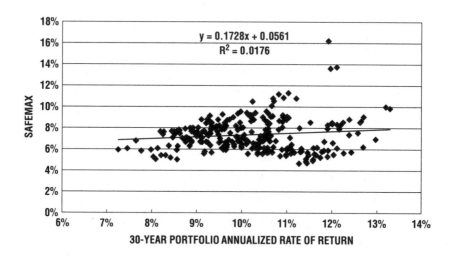

Rebalancing appears to account for the much higher portfolio returns experienced in practice vs. preliminary expectations. Mystery solved.

Do you sense a contradiction here? Earlier, I concluded that rebalancing was, on average, not crucial to retirees. Yet, I have just concluded that rebalancing was essential to generate higher investment returns. Does this make you want to return this book for credit?

Please, don't do that! My earlier conclusion was that rebalancing has little effect on *withdrawal rates* for most retirees. My most recent conclusion was that rebalancing is important for higher *investment returns*. As per Figure 9.5, investment returns have only a weak positive correlation with withdrawal rates; they are not the only factor affecting them. Inflation, for example, can exert a powerful influence on withdrawal rates through the expansion of dollar withdrawals. Thus, one can have a high investment return and a relatively low safe withdrawal rate. My two statements are not contradictory. Only confusing. Sorry!

CHAPTER 10

ELEMENT #7: THE "SUPERINVESTOR" – STRIVING FOR ABOVE-MARKET RETURNS

A re you an acolyte of Warren Buffett? Or are you a fan of "Roaring Kitty?" Either way, you probably believe you can, in a phrase, "beat the market." You're confident that you are a skillful investor who can consistently earn investment returns that outstrip the majority of mutual funds and exchange-traded funds (by the way, can I have your phone number?). In this chapter, we'll examine how earning returns that deviate from those posted by index funds affect SAFEMAX.

As mentioned in earlier chapters, a significant assumption underlying my research is that your retirement portfolio is invested in index funds, which seek to track precisely the returns of some class of investment. Many such funds track every imaginable (and obscure) index, such as the S&P 500, the Dow Jones Industrials, gold, international stocks, commodities, bitcoin, etc. Because of today's very low index fund management expenses, and the evaporation of commissions on trades, as an investor, you can be virtually assured of matching your index, year after year, with great precision.

I've chosen this approach because it's well-established that most "active" fund managers fail to beat their target index; as a result, passively managed index funds have become increasingly popular. Individual investors seem to fare even worse, as they are often scared out of the markets at the wrong time and miss out on juicy returns. Thus, my entire methodology is based on a buy-and-hold approach employing index funds, which, if followed with discipline, should help to produce those higher withdrawal rates we all seek.

However, the temptation to achieve higher-than-index returns, and therefore higher withdrawal rates, is irresistible for many. A few managers appear to possess the talent to achieve superior returns consistently. Consequently, I felt it would be remiss not to include a chapter on the rewards (and risks) of attempting to be a "superinvestor."

To study this issue, I'll focus on the "average SAFEMAX" retiree, as exemplified by the individual who retired on 1 July 1989. We'll use the "standard configuration" including a 30-year planning horizon, a fixed 55%/40%/5% stock/bond/cash allocation with the five equity classes equally weighted, a tax-advantaged account, and annual rebalancing. For simplicity of analysis, I'll also assume that the annual return of every stock asset class is increased or decreased from index levels in increments of 0.25%. The same increment will apply to all five stock asset classes simultaneously. Returns from bond funds will not be altered; bonds are generally much more difficult instruments from which to derive substantial above-market returns.

Figure 10.1 SAFEMAX vs. equity incremental investment returns (1 July 1989 retiree). Standard configuration, seven asset classes.

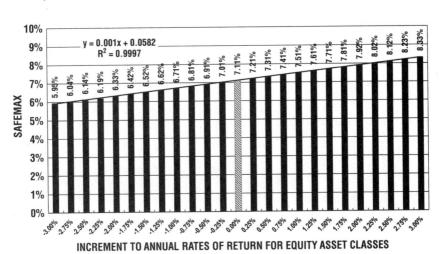

Figure 10.1 displays the results of our experiment. Unsurprisingly, the chart confirms that when investment returns increase, SAFEMAX increases, and when investment returns decrease, SAFEMAX declines. I have shown both sides of the coin here, as it is essential to remember that there are risks and rewards when attempting to improve index fund investment returns. If you fall short of expectations, you may pay the price in diminished withdrawal performance during retirement.

In the center of the chart is the SAFEMAX of 7.11% earned by our portfolio without any adjustments to equity returns. To the right of the center bar is SAFEMAX, produced by stronger-than-index returns. For example, the bar for +1.00% equity returns (i.e., each of the five equity asset classes has 1% added to their annual historical returns for every year) corresponds to a SAFEMAX of 7.51%. That's about a 5½% improvement over SAFEMAX for unadjusted equity returns. Are you disappointed that it's not higher? Remember that equities, the only asset classes whose returns were augmented, represent only 55% of the portfolio. Fixed income returns were not altered.

Figure 10.2 SAFEMAX vs. equity incremental investment returns (1 October 1968 retiree). Standard configuration, seven asset classes.

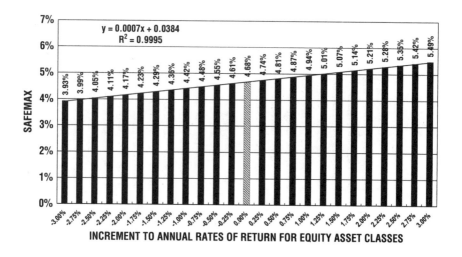

To the left of the center bar is SAFEMAX produced by weaker-than-index returns. The bar for −1.00% equity returns corresponds to a SAFEMAX of 6.71%, about 5½% below the "standard" SAFEMAX. The entire chart is symmetrical around the central bar, and a straight line accurately represents the relationship between incremental equity returns and SAFEMAX. The formula for the line appears on the chart.

Next, look at Figures 10.2 and 10.3, which display the same information for a low SAFEMAX (1 October 1968 retiree) and a high SAFEMAX (1 January 1975 retiree), respectively. The charts have very much the same shape. They are very linear, but, because we are beginning with different levels of SAFEMAX for index-only returns (central bar in each chart), the SAFEMAX for all the other data points are also different.

There is considerable uniformity in one aspect of these three figures: the same increment in returns produces approximately the same percentage change in SAFEMAX. Thus, as an example, for each of the three retirees, a +1.00% increment in returns produces about a 5% increase in SAFEMAX.

Figure 10.3   SAFEMAX vs. equity incremental investment returns (1 January 1975 retiree). Standard configuration, seven asset classes.

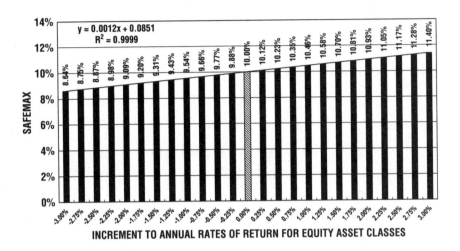

It should be clear from examining the figures in this chapter that attempts at superior investment returns can cut both ways. Failure to achieve the goal of higher returns – and even worse, generating sub-index returns – can result in a healthy hit to SAFEMAX and your retirement lifestyle. In a later chapter, we'll discuss how the goal of higher returns (and higher SAFEMAX) might be achieved not through individual stock selection or market timing but through risk management.

CHAPTER 11

ELEMENT #8: TIMING OF WITHDRAWALS

'm going to date myself now. I was trained as a financial planner using a Hewlett-Packard 12C calculator. This was the technology of choice in the late 1980s and early 1990s. It fit neatly into the palm of your hand and had four rows of tiny buttons. They still produce them, and on occasion, I still use mine. It's hard to teach an old dog new tricks, especially when the old tricks still get results.

You can perform all manner of computations on an HP12C. One of my favorite calculations was comparing the "present value" of a stream of monthly payments made at the beginning of the month with payments made at the end. This could represent mortgage payments made by you or, in the other direction, annuity payments made to you by an insurance company. Or, it could represent monthly withdrawals from a retirement account. *Hmmm.*

For example, you can enter annual payments of $10,000, with an annual interest rate of 6%, over a period of 10 years. But before you solve for the present value of those payments – which is the lump sum you'd need to generate those payments over the time selected at the interest rate specified – you must press either the "BEG" (BEGinning of the year payment) button or the "END" (END of the year payment) button. The BEG solution for present value is $139,716, while the END solution is $131,808. Why is there such a difference between the two?

The explanation is that we are encountering our old friend, the time value of money. If you receive your $10,000 annual payment on 1 January, the beginning of the year, you could invest it for a whole year at 6%, which effectively increases the monetary value of that payment to you. But if you receive your $10,000 on 31 December, there is no time to earn additional interest. Plus, you'd be too busy blowing a kazoo for New Year's Eve!

It's easy to confirm that same effect on SAFEMAX. For example, let's use our Universal SAFEMAX 1 October 1968 retiree with the standard configuration. If they withdrew their total annual amount on 1 January of each year for thirty years from a tax-advantaged account, their SAFEMAX would have been 4.45%. Had they waited until 31 December of each year to withdraw (really pushing the limits of the required minimum distribution rules!) SAFEMAX would have been 4.90%. That's more than 10% higher! Withdrawing money in an evenly distributed manner, of course, produces a 4.7% SAFEMAX.

The same 10%+ gain applies to my entire database of 269 "stalwart" retirees, although there are significant fluctuations from retiree to retiree. Those retirees fortunate to begin retirement in an extended bull market had higher percentage gains, while those who experienced early bear markets usually had lower percentage gains. However, the explanation remains: late withdrawals permit longer compounding, greater wealth accumulation, and often higher withdrawal rates.

Of course, this is not an argument for when to make withdrawals. From personal experience I assure you that retirees take money out when they need it! However, an individual may have valid personal reasons for deviating from an evenly distributed withdrawal strategy.

For example, an individual may plan to make all their retirement withdrawals from a traditional IRA account. By waiting till the end of each year to make their withdrawal, they permit the amount of that withdrawal to compound tax-free for almost a full year, marshaling the time-value-of-money forces to their benefit.

Of course, that would require that, in the first year, the individual have funds from another source to supply their withdrawals, such as a taxable account. After the first year, the following year's spending is covered by withdrawals from the IRA account made at the very end of the prior year. But that's not so hard to imagine, is it?

My emphasis in his book has been, and will continue to be, almost exclusively on evenly distributed withdrawals; this may be my last mention of any alternative approach. However, the alternative remains a valid possibility, and we should recognize it to properly accommodate it when one blue moon pops over the horizon.

CHAPTER 12

CREATING AND MANAGING A PERSONAL RETIREMENT WITHDRAWAL PLAN (FIVE CASE STUDIES)

n the preceding chapters, we've examined the eight Elements of a personal retirement withdrawal plan. We've studied how changing each of the Elements, plus inflation and stock market valuation, impacts your personal

SAFEMAX (first-year withdrawal rate). Now it's time to "put it all together" and construct some sample withdrawal plans to illustrate the application of all the concepts we've discussed.

We'll proceed by creating five sample plans for five hypothetical retirees. We'll also study how to manage those same five plans during retirement. Failure to properly manage a plan can yield poor results, even if the original plan was sound.

12.1 WITHDRAWAL PLAN #1

Creating a withdrawal plan is accomplished in three straightforward steps:

1. Select options for each of the eight Elements.
2. Determine both the current Shiller CAPE and inflation regime, and use them to select SAFEMAX (from the SAFEMAX finder tables).
3. Create a template chart as a measuring stick for your plan.

Our first task is the selection of options for each of the eight fundamental plan Elements. Table 12.1 contains the choices made by our hypothetical retiree #1.

The table options coincide with our "standard configuration" for the 4.7% rule. Nothing exotic here! As can be gleaned from the table, this individual is primarily interested in generating a stream of income from their investments during retirement, which will keep pace with inflation, as measured by CPI. They have no heirs and have no interest in leaving a legacy. Their life expectancy is 20 years, but to provide a margin of error in their plan, they have adopted a 30-year planning horizon. They will make all their withdrawals from a traditional IRA account.

Table 12.1   Elements for Retiree #1

Element	Option Selected
#1: Withdrawal scheme	COLA
#2: Planning horizon	30 years
#3: Taxable vs. non-taxable portfolios	Non-taxable (IRA)
#4: Leaving a legacy to heirs	None
#5: Asset allocation	Fixed 55% stocks/40% bonds/5% US Treasury Bills (five stock classes equally weighted @ 11%)
#6: Portfolio rebalancing frequency	1 year
#7: The "Superinvestor"	Not applicable; accepts "market" returns
#8: Withdrawal timing	Equally spaced during the year

Next, we will determine SAFEMAX for our retiree. As we discovered in Chapter 2, SAFEMAX is closely related to two factors: stock market valuation (Shiller CAPE) and inflation (CPI) regime, both at the time of retirement. The second metric, the inflation regime, is the most difficult of the two to pin down, as it involves an element of prediction. John Kenneth Galbraith, the famed economist, once stated, "The only function of economic forecasting is to make astrology look respectable." By the way, what's your sign?

The difficulty of forecasting CPI is further underscored by recent experience. We have witnessed CPI rise from 1.2% in 2020 to 8.0% in 2022, then fall to under 3% in late 2024. This volatility hardly buttresses confidence in forecasting economic variables! Nonetheless, we forge on, conscious that this may be a significant source of error in establishing SAFEMAX.

Our sample retiree estimates that CPI will average 3.5% over the first five years of his retirement, placing it in the "moderate inflation" category (between 2.5% and 5%). That means they will use Table 2.3 to select SAFEMAX.

The second factor, Shiller CAPE, is readily available from various sources, including the following website: https://www.multpl.com/shiller-pe. We learn that the retiree's Shiller CAPE is 14.8. Since the long-term average is about 17, stock prices were relatively cheap when they retired. That augurs well for our retiree because low stock prices generally mean there is a low risk of a major bear market early in retirement, which could negatively impact SAFEMAX.

Referring to Table 2.3, we find that a Shiller CAPE of 14.8 yields a SAFEMAX of 7.24%. That is a tad higher than the average SAFEMAX for all retirees (through 1 January 2013). But it is undoubtedly much better than would be expected from "the 4.7% rule"! Table 12.2 summarizes our computations for SAFEMAX.

Table 12.2 SAFEMAX for retiree #1

Inflation regime	3.5% (moderate inflation)
Source for data on investment returns and CPI	Hypothetical
Shiller CAPE	14.8
SAFEMAX (from Table 2.3)	7.24%

12.2 THE CURRENT WITHDRAWAL RATE, A POWERFUL TOOL

The final step in the development of our retirement withdrawal plan is to create a template chart using the Current Withdrawal Rate (CWR) metric. A template is a powerful tool for the management of a withdrawal plan. CWR is simply a percentage computed each year by dividing the dollar amount of that year's withdrawal by the portfolio value at the start of the year. For example, if you withdrew $50,000 during a year, and your portfolio began the year with a total value of $1 million, your CWR for that year would be 5.0%.

For the first year, CWR and IWR (initial withdrawal rate) are identical, as a matter of definition. After the first year, CWR will fluctuate as both dollar withdrawals and portfolio value vary. Over time (assuming you have selected to end your plan with a zero balance), CWR will eventually climb toward 100%, as during the last year, you will withdraw your entire remaining portfolio balance.

By way of illustration, Figure 12.1 displays the year-by-year values of CWR for the 1 July 1989 retiree, who sports a historically about-average 7.11% SAFEMAX (based on the standard configuration). The bar on the far left of the chart, which represents the first year of retirement, is equal to the retiree's SAFEMAX of 7.11%. CWR remains relatively steady around this value until the 13th year, after which it begins a steep, if uneven, climb. The final value in year 30 is 100%, as the planning horizon is 30 years, when all the portfolio's assets are scheduled to be consumed. Years beyond 27 are not shown, as they would dramatically distort the chart's scale.

Figure 12.1   Annual CWR for 1 July 1989 retiree. Standard configuration, seven asset classes.

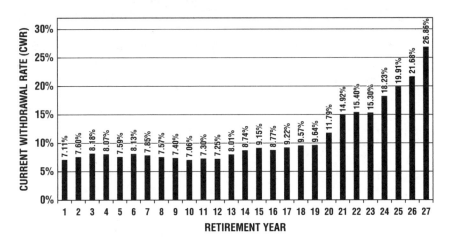

Virtually all historical CWR charts have this appearance, generally concave upwards, increasing from SAFEMAX at the left to 100% on the far right (unless the retiree specifies a legacy for heirs, in which case the value in year 30 will be less than 100%). It's not a smooth curve, as portfolio returns vary from year to year, particularly during stock bear markets.

The effects of bear markets are clear in Figure 12.1. The 1 July 1989 retiree experienced three such events during their 30-year tenure, in 2000, 2000–2002, and 2007–2009. The bear markets are all marked by a significant jump in CWR, as the portfolio shrinks in value while dollar withdrawals continue to increase. The effects of bear markets on CWR are generally delayed by one year, as CWR is computed from portfolio value at the beginning of the current year, which equals the value at the end of the prior year.

CWR measures how rapidly your investment "balloon" is being "deflated" at any point in time. This ratio is much more helpful in identifying problems than knowing the portfolio value or the dollar withdrawal amount alone.

12.3   THE SYNTHETIC CWR TEMPLATE

CWR can be used to measure your withdrawal plan's annual status. To do so, we need to develop a "CWR template chart" that establishes annual targets for your personal CWR. Comparing the actual CWR of your portfolio to the template CWR on a year-by-year basis will determine if your plan is "on track."

What could serve as a CWR template? The first possibility is to use a historical chart, such as Figure 12.1, for the 1 July 1989 retiree. If your personal SAFEMAX and CPI regime match those of the 1 July 1989 retiree, it seems reasonable that your personal CWR chart would also match its CWR chart closely.

I initially began by using this approach and included on Tables 2.2, 2.3, and 2.4 an additional column listing a historical retirement date, which could serve as a template. However, several problems developed with this methodology. First, locating a historical retiree with a closely matching SAFEMAX was not always possible. One could use a CWR curve for a historical retiree with a SAFEMAX which was "approximately the same" as your own, hoping that would be "close enough." However, that willy-nilly approach made me uncomfortable.

Second, each historical CWR curve contains fluctuations due to randomly occurring bear markets. To use the historical curve, one would have to know the exact timing, depth, and duration of each bear market so they could be accounted for when compared to your personal CWR curve. I felt this led to unnecessary complexity and cause for error.

As an alternative, I developed the concept of a "synthetic CWR curve," which was customizable for everyone. The synthetic curve doesn't represent the experience of any historical retiree. It's an artificial device based on a portfolio of assets that earn, every year, exactly their historical average long-term return (for example, as per Table 8.2, 10.1% per year for US Large-Company Stocks, 11.8% for US Small-Company Stocks, etc.). Inflation, as specified by the retiree (3.5% in our current example), would remain the same yearly. The value of the synthetic CWR in the first year of retirement would be the SAFEMAX selected from the table. The value of the last year's CWR would, by definition, be 100%, assuming a zero legacy.

But our design work is not quite finished. For the synthetic template, starting at the desired SAFEMAX and using average rates of return and average rates of inflation still doesn't guarantee a 100% CWR at the end of the planning horizon. Another feature is required: adjusting the returns of each of the five equity classes. This "returns dial" increases or decreases the annual return of each of the five equity classes by the same amount and can be "turned" to the required setting to ensure the template ends up at a 100% CWR. By arbitrary decision, bond and cash returns are not included in this adjustment, as they are generally much lower and more stable than equity returns.

12.4   SYNTHETIC CWR TEMPLATE FOR RETIREE #1

Figure 12.2 displays the synthetic CWR curve for retiree #1, incorporating all the mentioned features. As intended, it is a smooth curve beginning at the left with the chosen SAFEMAX of 7.24%. There are no "bumps" or "dips," as unlike a real-world curve, there are no bear or bull markets to cause them. CWR increases gradually in the early retirement years, then begins an increasingly steep climb in the later years. As before, only the first 27 years are shown, to avoid distortion in the scale of the graph.

Figure 12.2   Synthetic CWR template for retiree #1, 7.24% SAFEMAX. Standard configuration, seven asset classes.

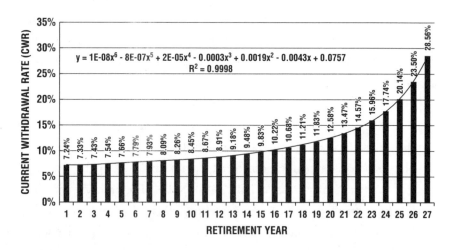

For reference, the "returns dial" was set at +0.72% to make the chart end at a 100% CWR. That means each of the five equity classes had 0.72% added to their returns yearly. This adjustment results in an average annual portfolio return of 9.8% each year, just slightly below the average for my entire retiree database.

Also noted in Figure 12.2 is a 6th-degree polynomial equation, which almost perfectly represents the values in the chart. If you have a math phobia, please relax! You don't have to solve an equation to make all this work. The chart supplies the annual values needed.

The personal retirement withdrawal plan for sample retiree #1 is now complete. It consists of the Element values in Table 12.1, the SAFEMAX factors in Table 12.2, and the synthetic CWR curve in Figure 12.2. In the next section, we'll "battle test" this plan to see how it fares during hypothetical retirement circumstances.

Before we do so, I can't fail to note the irony that we used average returns and average CPI to develop our synthetic CWR curve. At the same time, my research screams loudly that using averages is a flawed method to generate SAFEMAX. It's ironic but not contradictory. The synthetic CWR curve provides a neutral backdrop against which the unpredictable fluctuations of our real-world portfolio can be measured and assessed. It's descriptive, but not prescriptive.

12.5 MANAGING A PERSONAL WITHDRAWAL PLAN

Because withdrawal plans are long-range constructs, they can be affected by unexpected conditions that arise during retirement. The longer your planning horizon, the more likely you'll encounter such issues. As noted earlier, our "two-factor model" for identifying SAFEMAX is imperfect; approximately 15–20% of these long-range plans will require some adjustment during retirement. About half of those will require a reduction in withdrawals, while the other half will present opportunities for increasing withdrawals.

Thus, your withdrawal plan must be ***actively managed***. There are three steps required to manage your plan:

Step #1: Monitor your plan: Periodically (most likely annually) review the status of your plan against a benchmark. In most cases, the benchmark I recommend is the synthetic CWR template we developed in the previous section. Compute your portfolio's CWR for the current year and compare it to the template CWR.

Step #2: Identify significant divergences: Note if there is a substantial divergence between your current CWR and the corresponding CWR from your template. If so, decide if this divergence demands corrective action. This will require some experience. The five case studies are designed to sharpen your judgment in this regard.

Step #3: Adjust your plan (if required): If the divergences you detected in step #3 merit action, adjust your plan, or scrap it altogether and replace it with a new one. Once again, the case studies contain examples showing how this might be accomplished.

We'll apply this management process to the five plans we develop in this chapter. Doing so will give you a flavor of the problems you might encounter with your plan and the types of corrective actions required. This knowledge is essential to the long-term success of your plan. It is as important as the construction of the plan itself.

12.6 MANAGING WITHDRAWAL PLAN #1 (EARLY BEAR MARKET)

As you may recall, Retiree #1 opted for a "Standard Configuration" withdrawal plan (see Table 12.1) with a 7.24% initial withdrawal rate. Figure 12.3 shows the hypothetical annual portfolio returns and inflation experienced during the first 10 years of their retirement.

As you can see, this retiree starts well, with good portfolio returns each of the first two years. However, stocks unexpectedly fall into a substantial bear market in year #3, which persists into year #4. Stocks make a robust recovery in year #5, and the next five years provide good portfolio returns. Inflation has been well-contained during the decade and has declined from "moderate" to "low" in the middle years.

Figure 12.3   Retiree #1- hypothetical portfolio returns and CPI. Standard configuration, seven asset classes, only first 10 years shown.

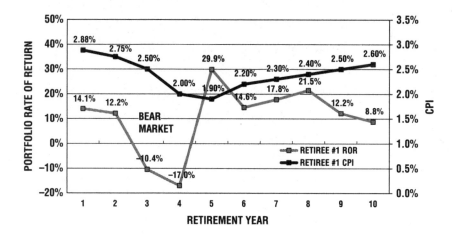

Figure 12.4   Current withdrawal rates for retiree #1, actual vs. template. Standard configuration, seven asset classes, first five years only.

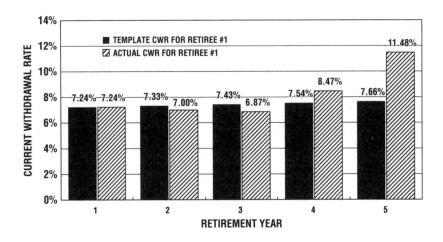

With five years of retirement behind them, we must now ask whether this retiree's plan is on track. Figure 12.4 shows the retiree's CWR template compared to the CWR calculated annually for their actual portfolio for the first five years of retirement. As a result of the bear market in years #2 and #3, the retiree's CWR has climbed well above the template CWR in year #5. What should they do about that?

Of all the management strategies one can think of, the simplest is to "do nothing." Let's begin with that. Figure 12.5 shows the consequences, after 10 years, of doing precisely that: nothing. As you can see, in years #6 through #10, the "CWR gap" between the template CWR and the actual CWR gradually closes, until in year #10, the retiree is only slightly behind plan. The "do nothing" strategy is a roaring success!

Of course, a powerful stock market recovery occurred after the rather nasty bear market in years #2 and #3. This is a perfectly typical scenario and to be expected. It illustrates that it is wrong to panic because your

Figure 12.5 Current withdrawal rates for retiree #1, actual vs. template. Standard configuration, seven asset classes, first 10 years, "do nothing."

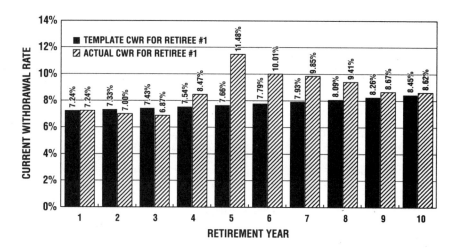

CWR temporarily rises above your template CWR. If the cause is a stock bear market, it's probably best to take no action and allow the subsequent market recovery to bring your plan back into register.

If good management always involved doing nothing, the world would be full of successful managers, I imagine. In the following case study, we encounter developments that demand immediate and forceful action.

12.7 WITHDRAWAL PLAN #2

As always, we begin constructing the plan with a selection of options for each of the eight fundamental plan Elements. Table 12.3 details the choices made by our hypothetical retiree #2.

Table 12.3   Elements for retiree #2

Element	Option Selected
#1: Withdrawal scheme	COLA
#2: Planning horizon	30 years
#3: Taxable vs. non-taxable portfolios	Non-taxable (IRA)
#4: Leaving a legacy to heirs	None
#5: Asset allocation	Fixed 55% stocks/40% bonds/5% US Treasury Bills (five stock classes equally weighted @ 11%)
#6: Portfolio rebalancing frequency	1 year
#7: The "Superinvestor"	Not applicable; accepts "market" returns
#8: Withdrawal timing	Equally spaced during the year

This retiree has also opted for the "standard configuration" of Elements. Our retiree estimates that CPI will average 4.0% over the first five years of their retirement, placing it in the "moderate inflation" category. However, this is higher than the average over the last 98 years (about 3.3%). That means they will also use Table 2.3 to select SAFEMAX.

Next, we learn that the Shiller CAPE on the retirement date is 22.3. Given the long-term average of about 17, this is an expensive stock market! Table 2.3 shows that a Shiller CAPE of 22.3 corresponds to a SAFEMAX of 5.54%. That is much lower than for retiree #1 and reflects the higher odds of a significant stock bear market early in retirement. Table 12.4 contains SAFEMAX and its determinants.

Table 12.4   SAFEMAX for retiree #2

Inflation regime	4% (moderate inflation)
Source for data on investment returns and CPI	Hypothetical
Shiller CAPE	22.3
SAFEMAX (from Table 2.2)	5.54%

Figure 12.6   Synthetic CWR template for retiree #2, 5.54% SAFEMAX. Standard configuration, seven asset classes.

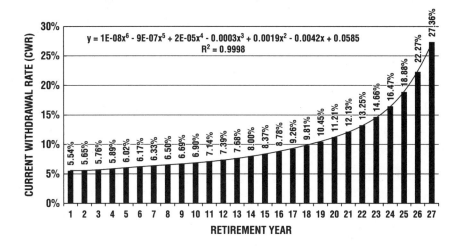

Finally, we derive the Synthetic CWR template for our sample retiree, which appears in Figure 12.6. A constant inflation rate of 4.0% is assumed throughout retirement, as per the instructions of the retiree, and average long-term historical rates of return for each asset class are used each year. An annual rate of return adjustment for equity asset classes of −0.15% is required to achieve a 100% withdrawal rate in year #30. The average annual portfolio rate of return is approximately 7.8%, well below the average for all retirees in my database. Only the first 27 years of the planning horizon are shown in the chart to avoid distortions.

This completes the plan for sample retiree #2. The documentation for the plan consists of Tables 12.3 and 12.4, as well as Figure 12.6. Next, let's see how their plan fared against hypothetical market conditions.

12.8   MANAGING WITHDRAWAL PLAN #2: UNEXPECTED HIGH INFLATION

Retiree #2 has opted for a "Standard Configuration" withdrawal plan with a 5.54% initial withdrawal rate. Figure 12.7 shows the hypothetical annual portfolio returns and inflation experienced during the first 10 years of their retirement.

The experience of retiree #2 is somewhat different from that of retiree #1. Their portfolios are hit in the third year by a major stock bear market that lasts two years. However, for retiree #2, inflation accelerates into the mid-single-digit range and remains elevated during the first 10 years. This creates a nasty environment for the retiree, requiring them to substantially increase their withdrawals each year. We would not be surprised to see the IR withdrawal plan encounter serious problems.

Figure 12.7   Retiree #2- hypothetical portfolio returns and CPI. Standard configuration, seven asset classes, only first 10 years shown.

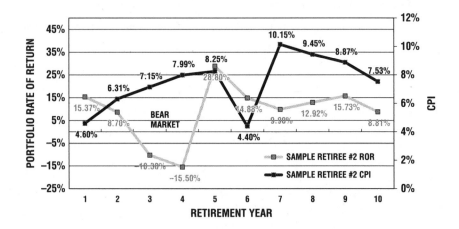

Figure 12.8 Current withdrawal rates for retiree #2, actual vs. template. Standard configuration, seven asset classes, first five years.

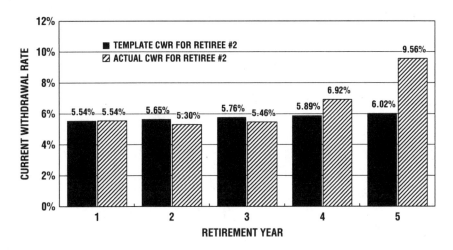

Figure 12.8 shows the CWR template of retiree #2 compared to the CWR calculated annually for their actual portfolio for just the first five years of retirement. This chart is, at first blush, quite similar to that of retiree #1. However, a warning sign is that the actual CWR seems to be pulling away from the template at a faster rate than for retiree #1.

With some misgivings, we decided to test the "do nothing" management approach again. Figure 12.9 shows the outcome, after 10 years, of such a laissez-faire tactic. The results are nothing short of catastrophic. There is no recovery in CWR, as there was for retiree #1. The actual CWR continues to diverge from its template counterpart, and in year #10, it is approaching 11%.

Clearly, not taking action is not an option! Withdrawals must be reduced. But by how much? Figure 12.10 shows the effects of reducing the dollar withdrawals in year #6 by an arbitrary 10%. That degree of reduction is not without pain, of course. But the outcome is disappointing: our CWR curve, although improved slightly, is still in runaway mode.

Figure 12.9   Current withdrawal rates for retiree #2, actual vs. template. Standard configuration, seven asset classes, first 10 years, "do nothing."

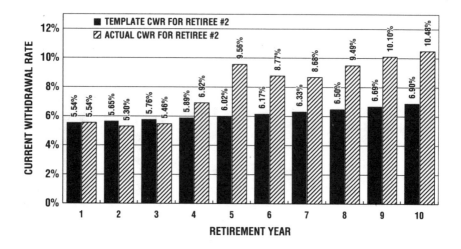

Figure 12.10   Current withdrawal rates for retiree #2, actual vs. template. Standard configuration, seven asset classes, first 10 years, "10% cut in year #6."

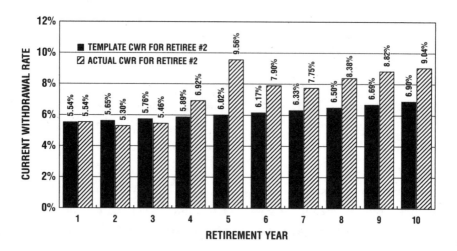

Figure 12.11 Current withdrawal rates for retiree #2, actual vs. template. Standard configuration, seven asset classes, first 10 years, "28% cut in year #6."

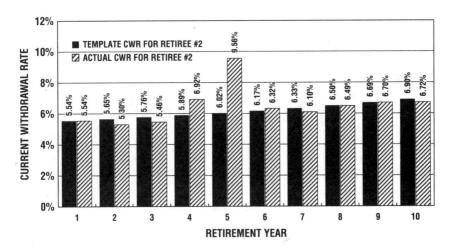

More draconian measures are indicated. In Figure 12.11, we apply a 28% reduction to dollar withdrawals in year #6. It looks as if we have finally rescued the withdrawal plan (at least through year #10) – but at what a terrible cost! Few retirees, I imagine, can cut their annual withdrawals by such a large percentage without significantly changing their lifestyle. But that is what is required, or the plan may collapse.

What if we had made changes earlier when we first received indications that inflation was running hotter than anticipated? Figure 12.12 shows the effects of implementing a 23% reduction in dollar withdrawals three years sooner – in year #3. At first, this doesn't seem much of an improvement, as the CWR values are about the same as in Figure 12.11 for years 7 through 10.

Figure 12.12   Current withdrawal rates for retiree #2, actual vs. template. Standard configuration, seven asset classes, first 10 years, "23% cut in year #3."

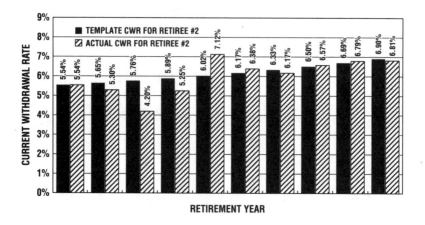

Figure 12.13   Comparison of withdrawals for "late" and "early" adjustments for retiree #2. Standard configuration, seven asset classes, first 10 years.

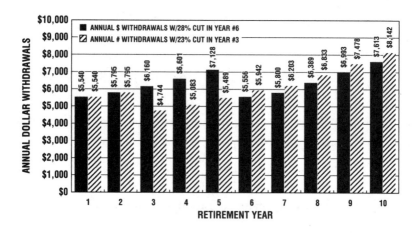

However, the benefits of this approach are more noticeable in Figure 12.13, which compares the actual dollar withdrawals for both strategies over the first 10 years. The total dollar withdrawals over the decade are approximately the same for both strategies, but note how the "early action" strategy improves results after year #6. This outcome is very important, as the 7% increase in dollar withdrawals is *permanent* and will also apply to all later years. This makes the "early action" strategy significantly superior over the long run. The improvement can be attributed directly to the capital preserved in years #3 through #5 because of reduced withdrawals.

Three significant lessons emerge from the study of this sample retiree:

1. High inflation is the retiree's great enemy, perhaps more so than the feared stock bear market. Bear markets are painful, but a recovery always follows them. Sustained inflation is even more painful because it elevates withdrawals permanently – when was the last time you can recall sustained *deflation?*

2. High inflation that threatens to endure must be dealt with in a draconian manner, with immediate steep withdrawal cuts. These cuts are likely to be permanent.

3. It is better to cut sooner rather than later in the face of sustained high inflation. Delays can be painful. Smaller cuts earlier are generally more effective than larger cuts later.

One more interesting question presents itself in this analysis. Obviously, the SAFEMAX of 5.54% selected by the retiree turned out not to be so "safe" after all! This was due almost entirely to the unexpected surge in inflation from the "moderate" regime to a "high" regime. Assuming, on the date of retirement, we had perfect foreknowledge of what would eventually happen to inflation, what "SAFEMAX" would we have chosen to produce a successful plan from the get-go?

The answer is: **4.60%**. Figure 12.14 illustrates how retiree #2 would have fared against the revised SAFEMAX, which is 17% less than the original not-so-SAFEMAX of 5.54%. In the early years, the lower SAFEMAX protected capital sufficiently, so the new CWR curve closely tracks the template curve in years #6 through #10. Of course, this says nothing about years #11 and beyond. Perhaps further adjustments may be required.

Figure 12.14   CWR comparison for template and optimized retiree #2. Standard configuration, seven asset classes, first 10 years.

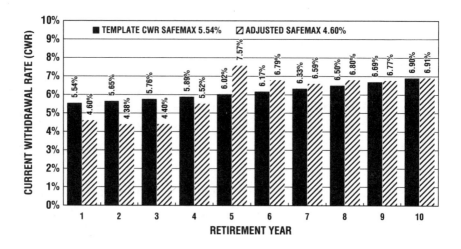

Did you catch it? We just broke the 4.7% rule! As you know, the worst-case Universal SAFEMAX of 4.7% was previously established (for this asset allocation) by the 31 October 1968 retiree. Apparently, the market circumstances retiree #2 faced in this hypothetical case study were worse than those endured by the 31 October 1968 retiree; 4.6% would be the new Universal SAFEMAX if this were a real-world outcome.

Fortunately, it's not. But in the years to come, who knows? Stay tuned!

12.9   WITHDRAWAL PLAN #3

In this case study, we'll depart from the "standard configuration" used in the first two case studies. Table 12.5 contains the "Element" choices of retiree #3.

Table 12.5   Elements for retiree #3

Element	Option Selected
#1: Withdrawal scheme	Front-loaded, 15% above SAFEMAX for the first 10 years (FL scheme)
#2: Planning horizon	40 years
#3: Taxable vs. non-taxable portfolios	Taxable (25% average ordinary income tax rate, 15% average capital gains tax rate)
#4: Leaving a legacy to heirs	$25,000 (in nominal terms) Starting value of portfolio = $100,000
#5: Asset allocation	Fixed 45% stocks/50% bonds/5% US Treasury Bills (five stock classes equally weighted @ 9%)
#6: Portfolio rebalancing frequency	1 year
#7: The "Superinvestor"	Not applicable; accepts "market" returns
#8: Withdrawal timing	Equally spaced during the year

That's different, isn't it? Given the long planning horizon, this might be a plan for an individual retiring early, perhaps about age 60. Or, perhaps, someone blessed with exceptional health. Also, for the first time, we encountered an individual who was not satisfied with the COLA method of withdrawals but wanted to spend at a higher rate earlier in retirement than cut back expenses in the eleventh year. As you may recall, I refer to this as the "Front-loaded" (FL) withdrawal scheme. Under FL, withdrawals increase annually with inflation, as in the COLA scheme, but there is a sharp "cliff" or drop-off in the eleventh year.

Another point of difference is that this individual insists that a "legacy" balance of at least $25,000 remain in their retirement account at the end of the 40-year planning horizon. The remaining $25,000 from a starting portfolio of $100,000 will not be worth much (in real terms) after 40 years of inflation, but clearly, they are thinking of someone. Perhaps they wish to leave their dog an exceptionally large chew toy!

Also, withdrawals will be made from a taxable account, not a tax-advantaged one. The average tax rate on ordinary income (federal + state + local) is specified at 25%, and the average capital gains tax was set at 15%. These are only preliminary estimates and are subject to change due to portfolio performance and the whims of Congress. Both, of course, are highly unpredictable.

Finally, this individual is a conservative investor and prefers a fixed allocation in equities of 45%, divided equally among our five asset classes (i.e., 9% in each). In Chapter 8 (Figure 8.2), we learned that this allocation to equities is at the lower end of a "plateau" over which SAFEMAX is virtually unchanged. The retiree will only pay a minor penalty in SAFEMAX for this conservative stance.

It's time to consider the retiree's inflation regime and Shiller CAPE to determine SAFEMAX. Table 12.6 contains the retiree's specifications for an annual inflation rate of 2% (low-inflation regime) for the duration of their retirement. This is lower than the 3.3% average for the last 100 years, but the retiree is confident a low-inflation environment will prevail. At the time of retirement, the Shiller CAPE is 18.0.

Table 12.6 SAFEMAX for retiree #3

Inflation regime	2% (moderate inflation)
Source for data on investment returns and CPI	1 October 1959 retiree
Shiller CAPE	18.00
COLA SAFEMAX (from Table 12.7)	4.09%

Note that four of the above deviations from the "standard configuration" (planning horizon, account type, asset allocation, and legacy) tend to drive SAFEMAX lower. To confirm this, consider Figure 12.15. The upper line is taken from Figure 2.8 and shows SAFEMAX vs. Shiller CAPE for all low-inflation retirees using the standard configuration. The lower line

Figure 12.15   SAFEMAX vs. Shiller CAPE (COLA standard configu-ration vs. retiree #3). Taxable account, 40 years longevity, seven asset classes, fixed 45%/50%/5% stocks/bonds/cash, only first 10 years shown.

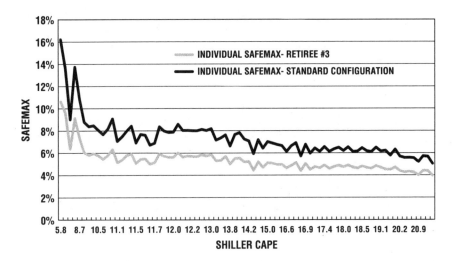

displays SAFEMAX vs. Shiller CAPE for retiree #3, using the options they chose for their Elements. SAFEMAX is, in all instances, much lower for our retirees. This confirms our expectations,

Wait a minute! Why are we looking at a COLA curve for our retiree? Didn't they opt for an FL withdrawal scheme? Yes, but recall that to give meaning to the FL scheme, we must first compute what the SAFEMAX would have been had we used the COLA scheme. Then, we can compute the "cliff" as a percentage reduction from the COLA SAFEMAX.

In Figure 12.16, we take the next step. We focus on just the COLA SAFEMAX data for our retiree and fit a mathematical curve to that data. The formula for that curve is shown on the chart. Math haters, don't panic! Using that curve, I have created Table 12.7, showing the COLA SAFEMAX values for various Shiller CAPE values. You will not have to perform any computations; it is just a simple "look-up" operation.

Figure 12.16 SAFEMAX vs. Shiller CAPE (retiree #3 using COLA). Taxable account, 40 years longevity, seven asset classes, fixed 45%/50%/5% stocks/bonds/cash, only first 10 years shown.

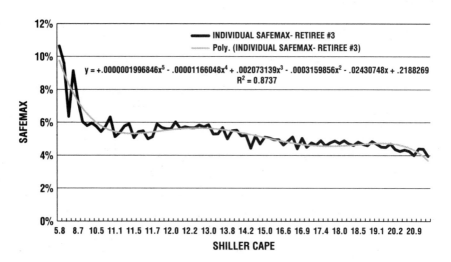

Table 12.7 SAFEMAX finder for retiree #3. 45% equities (9% each)/ 50% bonds/5% cash $25,000 legacy, 40-year planning horizon, Low-Inflation Regime (CPI between +0.0% and +2.49%).

Beginning Shiller CAPE	Curve-fitted SAFEMAX
6.00 to 6.49	8.93%
6.50 to 6.99	8.27%
7.00 to 7.49	7.68%
7.50 to 7.99	7.15%
8.00 to 8.49	6.68%
8.50 to 8.99	6.27%
9.00 to 9.49	5.92%
9.50 to 9.99	5.62%
10.00 to 10.49	5.36%
10.50 to 10.99	5.15%
11.00 to 11.49	4.98%

Beginning Shiller CAPE	Curve-fitted SAFEMAX
11.50 to 11.99	4.84%
12.00 to 12.49	4.72%
12.50 to 12.99	4.64%
13.00 to 13.49	4.57%
13.50 to 13.99	4.51%
14.00 to 14.49	4.47%
14.50 to 14.99	4.43%
15.00 to 15.49	4.39%
15.50 to 15.99	4.36%
16.00 to 16.49	4.32%
16.50 to 16.99	4.27%
17.00 to 17.49	4.22%
17.50 to 17.99	4.16%
18.00 to 18.49	4.09%
18.50 to 18.99	4.01%
19.00 to 19.49	3.93%
19.50 to 19.99	3.85%
20.00 to 20.49	3.77%
20.50 to 20.99	3.70%
21.00 to 21.49	3.65%
21.50 to 21.99	3.62%

We can now look up in Table 12.7 the Shiller CAPE of 18.0 and discover it is associated with a SAFEMAX of 4.09%. This seems low compared to our previous case studies, but remember that this individual has accepted values for the Elements that depress SAFEMAX. Table 12.7 is a "custom job" created just for this individual and their specifications. This will always be required when the chosen Elements differ from those in the standard configuration.

Figure 12.17 Synthetic CWR template for retiree #3. 4.70% IWR, FL scheme, 40 year horizon, taxable (25% OI, 15% CG), 2% inflation, seven asset classes, 45%/50%/5% stocks/bonds/cash.

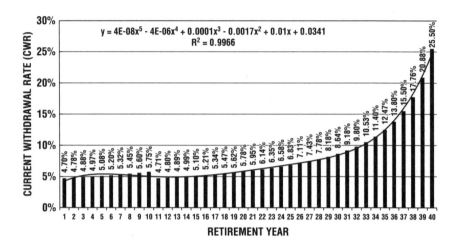

Our final task in creating the withdrawal plan is establishing the CWR template for retiree #3. Per the specs, the template will be based on constant 2% inflation. Investment returns will utilize historical average rates of return, but our "returns dial" calls for a downward adjustment of about −0.67% for each equity asset class each year. Our initial withdrawal rate, as specified, will be 15% of the COLA SAFEMAX of 4.09%, or 4.704%. Mixing all these ingredients, we discover that a cliff reduction in withdrawals of −20.5% is required in year #11 so that a balance of $25,000 remains in the account at the end of year #40. The final template curve appears in Figure 12.17.

Note that all 40 years of the plan are shown in the chart. We showed less than the full horizon in the prior two case studies, as a CWR of 100% in the final year would have grossly distorted the chart's scale. In this case, the CWR in the last year is only about 25%, as we are not spending the whole account; we are leaving a $25,000 legacy balance. This plan could continue for an additional four years if necessary. In effect, the provision for a legacy gives the retiree a "hedge" against an unexpectedly long life.

Figure 12.18 "Cliff %" required for given IWR, "front-loaded" scheme (three retirees, taxable), 40 years longevity, taxable account (25%OI /15%CG), 5% TB, 40% ITGB, 55% stocks equal-weighted, $5,000 legacy

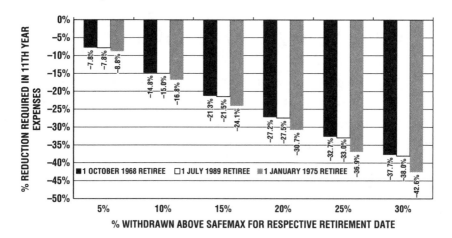

The 20.5% cliff is evident in Figure 12.17, as CWR drops by more than a full percentage point. "Is this cliff steep enough to do the job?" you might ask. If you recall, we examined some sample cliff percentages back in Chapter 4, specifically in Figure 4.6. For an initial "ramp" above SAFEMAX of 15%, the cliffs in that chart were 27% or more, and here we are utilizing only a 20.5% cliff.

To provide some comfort, I have re-computed Figure 4.6 in Figure 12.18, using the same three sample historical retirees but employing the Elements and preferences of retiree #3. As you can see, in all cases, the cliff is much smaller for our current retiree. The effects of a longer planning horizon, taxable vs. tax-advantaged account, etc., militate to favor a smaller cliff. This underscores how much withdrawal plans can differ from one individual to another. One size certainly does not fit all.

Our withdrawal plan for this retiree is now complete. Well, that was a bit of work! This is an exceptionally complex plan with a lot of moving parts. Let's see how it fared over the years.

12.10 MANAGING WITHDRAWAL PLAN #3 (FRONT-LOADED WITHDRAWAL SCHEME)

In previous case studies, I used hypothetical data for the retiree's investment returns and inflation to make specific points about plan management. For this case study, we will supply our retiree with the actual investment returns and CPI performance experienced by the 1 October 1959 retiree. Their starting SAFEMAX (4.11%) and early low-inflation performance closely match the retiree's specifications. The annual returns and CPI data appear in Figure 12.19 for all 40 years of the plan.

Figure 12.19   Retiree #3 – portfolio returns and CPI (based on 1 October 1959 retiree), seven asset classes, fixed 45%/50%/5% stocks/bonds/cash

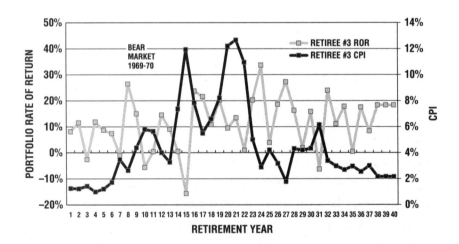

Figure 12.20   Current withdrawal rates for retiree #3, actual vs. template. FL scheme, taxable account, 40 years longevity, seven asset classes, fixed 45%/50%/5% stocks/bonds/cash.

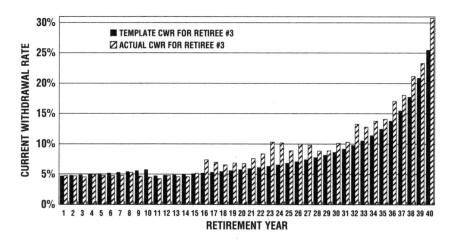

As you can see from the figure, retiree #3 begins their retirement in fine style. They don't experience a severe bear market (the 1973–1974 event) until year #14. Inflation over the first 10 years averages 2.4%, just slightly more than expected but still fitting our definition of "low." Some clouds are on the horizon, though; notice how inflation accelerates in year #10 and beyond, achieving double-digit levels in at least four years. This will certainly impact the plan mid-retirement.

Figure 12.20 compares the CWR curve for our retiree with their template. As expected, the early years are favorable. For the first 14 years, the retiree's CWR is "below plan," less than the template's. In year #11, CWR for both takes a sharp drop due to the 20.5% cliff mandated by the plan.

However, something critical happens in year #15. A combination of a −16% portfolio loss with almost 12% inflation causes the CWR to surge above its template. For the remainder of the planning horizon, actual CWR remains above template; but it's important to note that *it does not run away from the template*. The difference between the two curves alternatively shrinks and swells and only becomes very large in the final year. However, the portfolio lasted the entire 40-year planning horizon. The CWR chart shows that a primary goal of the plan, 40-year portfolio longevity, has been satisfied.

This is one case, however, where the CWR chart doesn't tell the whole story. That's because, in addition to our goal to have the portfolio last 40 years, we have another goal: a minimum of a $25,000 balance in the account at the end of year #40. To verify this was accomplished, consider Figure 12.21, which lists the year-end portfolio value for both the template and our retiree during each of the forty years.

Are you surprised by this chart? Look at the amazing growth of the portfolio in years 17 through 29! It completely outstrips the template. This is the result of solid investment returns after the 1973–1974 bear market. Eventually, the actual portfolio value turns downward, but the "terminal value" exceeds $50,000, more than double our target. This plan has enjoyed a rousing success, with no adjustments required to be made.

Figure 12.21 Year-end portfolio value for retiree #3, actual vs. template. FL scheme, taxable account, 40 years longevity, seven asset classes, fixed 45%/50%/5% stocks/bonds/cash.

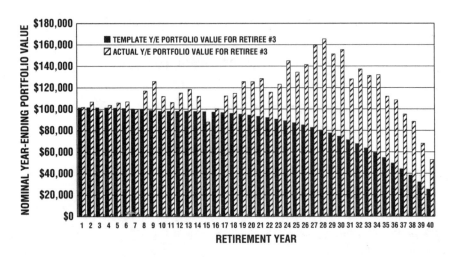

What lessons can we learn from the performance of this plan? There are several:

1. A retirement portfolio with a strong start in its first 10 years (in both investment returns and inflation) can withstand a lot of adverse circumstances in its later years, even without adjustment. Even the terrible 1973–1974 stock bear market and high inflation of the 1970s couldn't sink this plan.

2. The Front-Loaded withdrawal scheme operated successfully in this case. It appears to be a viable approach to withdrawing money during retirement. Presumably, our retiree was well prepared for the 20.5% haircut in year #11!

3. The CWR curve is a powerful tool, but it may need to be supplemented by other tools, such as a chart of annual portfolio values, to determine a plan's success completely.

Finally, the approximately $50,000 balance remaining in the account at the end of 40 years was, after years of high inflation, equivalent in value to only $8,735 at the start of retirement.

Maybe they'll settle for a small chew toy.

This was a challenging withdrawal plan to construct and analyze. I promise the following two case studies will be more straightforward but with no less profound conclusions.

12.11 WITHDRAWAL PLAN #4

Our first task is the selection of options for each of the eight fundamental plan Elements. Table 12.8 contains the choices made by our hypothetical retiree.

Table 12.8   Elements for retiree #4

Element	Option Selected
#1: Withdrawal scheme	COLA
#2: Planning horizon	30 years
#3: Taxable vs. non-taxable portfolios	Non-taxable (Roth IRA)
#4: Leaving a legacy to heirs	None
#5: Asset allocation	Fixed 55% stocks/40% bonds/5% US Treasury Bills (five stock classes equally weighted @ 11%)
#6: Portfolio rebalancing frequency	1 year
#7: The "Superinvestor"	Not applicable; accepts "market" returns
#8: Withdrawal timing	Equally spaced during the year

Once again, we return to our standard configuration of the COLA withdrawal scheme, tax-advantaged account, and the other usual suspects for this retiree. This permits us to use Tables 2.2, 2.3, and 2.4 to establish our SAFEMAX.

This retiree has determined they will be in a "moderate inflation regime" in their early retirement years. An average inflation rate of 3.0% will be used to compute the synthetic CWR curve template. This percentage is close to the nearly 100-year statistical average for CPI.

Table 2.3 for moderate inflation thus applies. At retirement, the Shiller CAPE is 18, also close to its historical average. This implies a "fairly valued" stock market. According to Table 2.3, a Shiller CAPE of 18 implies a SAFEMAX of 7.26%. A summary of the SAFEMAX appears in Table 12.9.

Table 12.9   SAFEMAX for retiree #4

Inflation regime	3% (moderate inflation)
Shiller CAPE	18
SAFEMAX (from Table 2.3)	7.26%

So far, nothing outlandish here. But surprising cakes often get baked in the market oven. Let's see what happens to our retiree.

12.12   MANAGING WITHDRAWAL PLAN #4 (SAVING THE BEST FOR LATER)

We'll use actual investment returns and CPI data from the 1 October 1989 retiree to represent the experience of retiree #4. The 1 October 1990 retiree is a close match in the inflation regime and Shiller CAPE to retiree #4. The CWR template appears in Figure 12.22. Figure 12.23 lists the investment returns and inflation experienced by retiree #4 during the first decade of their retirement,

Figure 12.22   Synthetic CWR template for retiree #4. 7.26% IWR, standard configuration, 3% inflation, seven asset classes.

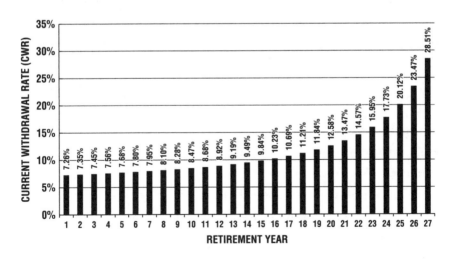

Figure 12.23 Retiree #4- portfolio returns and CPI (based on 1 October 1990 retiree). Standard configuration, seven asset classes, first 10 years.

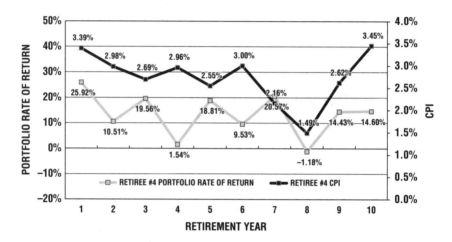

As per Figure 12.23, retiree #4 begins retirement auspiciously. Portfolio returns over the first 10 years exceed 13% annually, and inflation averages less than 3%. This is truly a "goldilocks" scenario for a retiree. It simply doesn't get much better than that!

In Figure 12.24, we observe the state of the retiree's plan against their template through the first 10 years of retirement. Because of their strong start, the retiree's actual CWR is well below that of the template. An increase in withdrawals seems justified. In year #5, actual CWR trails template CWR by 20%. Let's increase the dollar withdrawals by 20% in the sixth year (and, consequently, all subsequent years).

Figure 12.25 takes a 15-year view of our adjustment to CWR in year #6. Surprisingly, it appears that it wasn't enough! In years #7 through #15, template CWR continues to outpace actual CWR by a wide margin. A second adjustment seems called for. In year #9, actual CWR trails the template by 18%. It was decided to further increase withdrawals by 10% in year #10.

Figure 12.24 Current withdrawal rates for retiree #4, actual vs. template FP scheme. Seven asset classes, first 10 years.

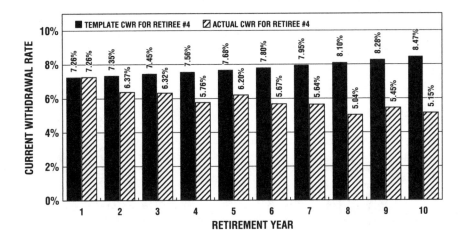

Figure 12.25 Current withdrawal rates for retiree #4, adjusted vs. template. Standard configuration, seven asset classes (increase withdrawals by 20% in year #6), first 15 years.

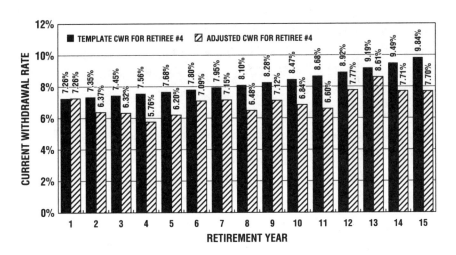

Figure 12.26 Current withdrawal rates for retiree #4, adjusted #2 vs. template. Standard configuration, seven asset classes (further increase withdrawals by 10% in year #10), first 27 years.

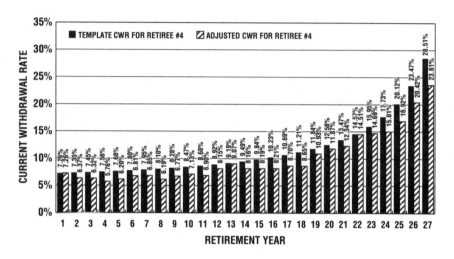

It seems as if there is room to do even more, don't you think? But things have gone so well for so long, and stock valuations have gotten so high, it seems appropriate to be a bit conservative. (The 1 October 1989 investor, as it turns out, was about to enter the dot.com bust and the ensuing nasty bear market of 2000–2002.) After all, we can always make additional adjustments in a few years if it seems appropriate!

Figure 12.26 depicts the effects of our two adjustments, almost to the end of the 30-year horizon. We've managed to close the gap between template and the actual CWR, but astonishingly, even more could have been done! I note that increasing in year #10 by 12% instead of 10% would have closed the gap completely, but who can predict that accurately? There is definitely room for another modest adjustment, perhaps in year #15.

What can we learn from this case study?

1. Not all adjustments to withdrawals are downward. If conditions are favorable, withdrawals may be increased.

2. Events later in retirement, if dramatic enough, can have a potent impact on the withdrawal plan. In this case, the Shiller CAPE rose from about 18 at retirement to over 37 at the end of 30 years (one of the most expensive stock markets in history). That's more than a doubling, and it provided a massive tailwind to investment returns. Who could have foreseen that at the outset?

3. Adjustments to the withdrawal plan can and probably should be made incrementally, particularly in response to outstanding investment performance. Looking back on this retiree, they could have withstood a single 30% withdrawal increase in year #5 instead of the 20% increase that was implemented. But that would have been greedy. The markets could have gone the other way.

12.13   WITHDRAWAL PLAN #5

Retiree #5 is intrigued by the "Fixed Percentage (FP)" withdrawal scheme. As you may recall, this scheme dictates a withdrawal each year equal to a fixed percentage of the portfolio value at the beginning of the year. Thus, withdrawals will fluctuate with portfolio value and can decline (or increase) significantly in any given year. Also, inflation has no direct impact on withdrawals using this scheme. Aside from the choice of withdrawal scheme, the retiree accepts all the standard values for the eight Elements, as per Table 12.10.

Table 12.10   Elements for retiree #5

Element	Option Selected
#1: Withdrawal scheme	Fixed Percentage of BOY portfolio value (FP scheme)
#2: Planning horizon	30 years
#3: Taxable vs. non-taxable portfolios	Tax-advantaged (Traditional IRA)
#4: Leaving a legacy to heirs	None
#5: Asset allocation	Fixed 55% stocks/40% bonds/5% US Treasury Bills (five stock classes equally weighted @ 11%)
#6: Portfolio rebalancing frequency	1 year
#7: The "Superinvestor"	Not applicable; accepts "market" returns
#8: Withdrawal timing	Equally spaced during the year

As you may recall, there is no "SAFEMAX" for the FP scheme, as theoretically, the portfolio never runs out of money (although the remaining balance could be measured just in pennies). Thus, we refer only to the Initial Withdrawal Rate (IWR).

This retiree is single and has considerable income from other sources. They intend that the withdrawals from their IRA account be used primarily for discretionary purposes and are not too concerned if the annual withdrawal amount fluctuates substantially. They also find it attractive that, under the FP system, their account might last well beyond their formal planning horizon if they live longer than expected.

In Chapter 4, we learned that total withdrawals for the FP scheme are maximized for IWRs between approximately 5.00% and 6.25%. Our retiree chooses a rate near the upper limit of this range, 6.00%. Although it has no impact on the withdrawal plan, a constant annual inflation rate of 3.0% is assumed to construct the template. This is summarized in Table 12.11. The retiree is aware that under the COLA system, the IWR might have been considerably higher (as it turns out, more than 8%), but they are satisfied by the trade-offs discussed above.

Table 12.11   WR for retiree #5

Inflation regime	Assume 3% annually for template
Source for data on investment returns and CPI	Not relevant
Shiller CAPE	Not relevant
Initial Withdrawal Rate (IWR)	6.00% (high end of the range for maximized total withdrawals)

A synthetic CWR curve is of little management value for this retiree, as CWR will be a constant 6% throughout retirement. In its place, in Figure 12.27, I introduce a synthetic Portfolio Value (PV) curve, which portrays the end-of-year portfolio value for all 30 years of the planning horizon. This should serve as an effective template against which to measure the performance of the retiree's actual plan. For this retiree, a constant CPI of 3%, close to the long-term historical average, is maintained. The "ROR dial" is set at +0.8% to generate an average portfolio return of 10%, matching the long-term average for all retirees in my database.

Figure 12.27   Synthetic portfolio value template for retiree #5, 6.0% IWR. FP scheme, tax-advantaged account, 30 years longevity, 3% inflation, seven asset classes, 55%/40%/5% stocks/bonds/cash.

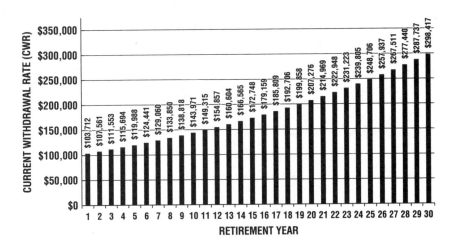

12.14 MANAGING WITHDRAWAL PLAN #5 (CHANGING HORSES MID-STREAM)

Arbitrarily, we shall use actual investment returns from the 1 January 1949 retiree to represent the experience of retiree #5. The 1 January 1949 retiree, using the FP scheme, experienced peak "total withdrawals" very near an IWR of 6.0%, which matches the preference of our retiree. Historical CPI data is irrelevant, as the withdrawal rate depends only on portfolio value, not inflation. The historical investment ROR profile for our retiree is shown in Figure 12.28. The 1 January 1949 retiree enjoyed annual portfolio returns exceeding 11% during its first 10 years, contributing to its COLA SAFEMAX of almost 8.5%. It was a great time to retire!

Figure 12.28   Retiree #5- portfolio returns (based on 1/1/1949 retiree). Seven asset classes, fixed 55%/40%/5% stocks/ bonds/cash.

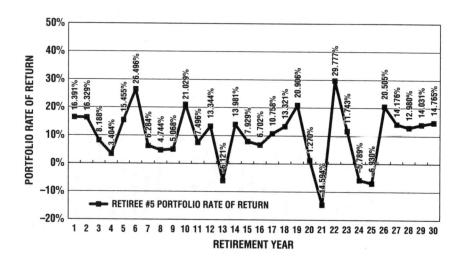

Figure 12.29   Portfolio value for retiree #5, actual vs. template. FP scheme, seven asset classes, 55%/40%/5% stocks/bonds/cash, first 9 years.

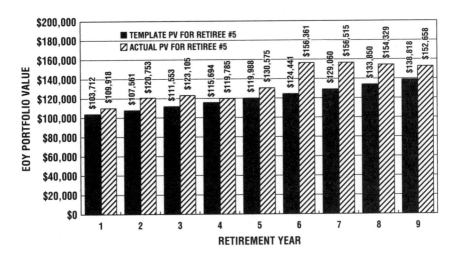

Figure 12.29 compares the retiree's actual end-of-year portfolio value vs. their template for the first nine years of retirement. As the actual portfolio value consistently exceeds the template's, this must be considered a successful plan with no apparent need for adjustment.

However, this is far from the end of the story! Toward the end of the ninth year, retiree #5 gets married. A larger home is under consideration. They reassess their income needs and decide they want a higher level of income that will keep pace with inflation. The FP scheme no longer provides the level and consistency of income they require in the future.

Is this a problem? Not really! *A withdrawal plan is not forever.* It can be modified, as in the previous four case studies. Or it can be scrapped completely and replaced with a new one, as we are about to do! This can occur at any point during retirement and be done multiple times, if necessary. I'd advise against doing it too frequently, though, as it then no longer becomes a plan but a plaything.

To create a new plan for retiree #5, we repeat the original process, beginning with the Elements. Table 12.12 shows the choices made by the retiree (and their new spouse!).

Table 12.12   Elements for retiree #5 (new plan)

Element	Option Selected
#1: Withdrawal scheme	COLA
#2: Planning horizon	30 years
#3: Taxable vs. non-taxable portfolios	Tax-advantaged (Traditional IRA)
#4: Leaving a legacy to heirs	None
#5: Asset allocation	Fixed 55% stocks/40% bonds/5% US Treasury Bills (five stock classes equally weighted @ 11%)
#6: Portfolio rebalancing frequency	1 year
#7: The "Superinvestor"	Not applicable; accepts "market" returns
#8: Withdrawal timing	Equally spaced during the year

Our retiree has converted to a "standard configuration" plan, including adoption of the COLA withdrawal scheme. Although nine years of their original 30-year planning horizon have been consumed, they opt for a full 30 years in the new plan. They justify this because there are now two lives to plan for, not just one, and there is a high probability that at least one of them will require the 30-year planning horizon.

Next, we consider both inflation and stock market valuation, using Table 2.3, to determine SAFEMAX. The outcome appears in Table 12.13.

Table 12.13   SAFEMAX for retiree #5 (new plan)

Inflation regime	3% (moderate inflation)
Shiller CAPE	13.8
SAFEMAX (from Table 2.3)	7.18%

Figure 12.30 Synthetic CWR template for retiree #5, 7.18% SAFEMAX, new plan. Standard configuration, 3% inflation, seven asset classes.

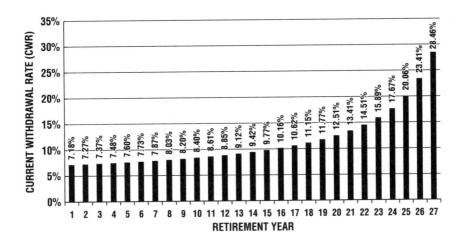

At a Shiller CAPE of 13.8, stocks are quite cheap, suggesting strong investment returns in the immediate years ahead. The corresponding SAFEMAX of 7.18%, from Table 2.2, is almost a 20% improvement from the retiree's current 6% withdrawal rate. This modification satisfies their desire for a higher level of income.

Using the COLA withdrawal scheme, a new template is now required, with a starting portfolio value that dovetails with the portfolio value at the end of the ninth year. Because we are now using the COLA scheme, we can revert to using the synthetic CWR curve. The new CWR template is shown in Figure 12.30. Note that the "ROR dial" is set to add 0.47% to the annual returns of each equity class so that the template lasts precisely 30 years.

For consistency, we shall continue to use the ROR data for the 1 January 1949 retiree as our "actual" performance. Because we have converted to the COLA scheme, we shall also use the CPI data from that retiree. Both metrics are shown in Figure 12.31 for the next 30 years of the plan.

Figure 12.31 Retiree #5 (new plan)- portfolio returns and CPI (based on 1 January 1949 retiree). Standard configuration, seven asset classes.

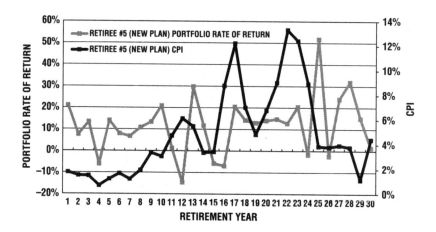

Figure 12.32 Current withdrawal rates for retiree #5, new plan, actual vs. template. Standard configuration, seven asset classes, (further increase withdrawals by 10% in year #10), first 26 years.

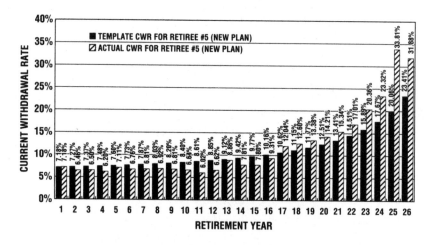

Finally, in Figure 12.32, we unveil the CWR curve for the new plan, and see how it stacks up against the template. The comparison through year #16 is very good, but in year #17, the actual CWR exceeds the template by ever-increasing amounts. The cause was the accelerating inflation of the 1970s, which was not anticipated in the withdrawal plan.

An adjustment should be made to the plan in the second half of retirement to protect against the effects of inflation. But you know how to do that by now, don't you?

There are several lessons to be learned from this case study:

1. No withdrawal plan has to last forever. It can be modified or completely changed at any time during retirement if it no longer meets your needs. Just don't do it too often!
2. If a new plan is adopted, the entire planning process should be repeated from the beginning. Don't take shortcuts!
3. A new plan can change any or all of the Elements of the original plan. It must also incorporate current stock market valuations, as well as a reassessment of the inflation regime.

Conclusion: I hope these five case studies have provided helpful guidance on managing your withdrawal plan during retirement. I've illustrated several variations, from simple adjustments to the withdrawal rate to wholesale replacement of one plan with an entirely different plan. One can't be sure what circumstances one will encounter during a lengthy retirement, but I believe the methodology I've provided has the flexibility to adapt to a wide range of different conditions.

CHAPTER 13

TOPICS OF SPECIAL INTEREST

I n this chapter, we'll discuss some interesting and useful topics that don't fit neatly into the subject matter of earlier chapters.

13.1   HAS THE 4.7% RULE ALREADY FAILED?

People have been predicting the demise of the "4% rule" (or the 4.7% rule, as you now know) ever since I wrote my first paper on the topic in 1994. It's the most common question I receive at presentations and in media interviews. To me, interest in it seems right up there with topics such as the shooter on the grassy knoll or whether Americans truly landed on the Moon in 1969.

This question has gained greater currency since several prominent parties in the financial world have recently maintained that much lower withdrawal rates are called for under current conditions of high stock market valuations and higher inflation. Rates as low as 3% have been suggested as more appropriate. Is there a reason for genuine concern here? Let's take a closer look.

To begin with, what do people mean when they ask, "Has the 4.7% rule failed?" This means that SAFEMAX for a recent retiree is lower than the worst-case Universal SAFEMAX by 4.7%. In other words, a new "worst-case" has developed. I certainly don't deny that's possible; as you know from Figure 2.2, Universal SAFEMAX has declined several times since 1926. It could certainly happen again.

The 4.7% Universal SAFEMAX works for all retirees through 1 January 1993. Could failure have occurred for a retiree in the intervening thirty-plus years?

At the outset, we should note that sufficient years must pass to ensure that any retiree's withdrawal plan has failed. That could be as long as 20 years or more. Therefore, it is a real stretch to claim that the withdrawal plan of anyone who retired over the last dozen years or so is certain to have failed. There just isn't enough information available to state that with assurance.

We can, however, examine the withdrawal plans of those who retired since 1 January 1993, which is beyond my "stalwart group" of 269 retirees who possess at least a full 30 years of data. One such example is the individual who retired on 1 July 2000.

This retiree is of particular interest as they retired at the beginning of a major stock bear market, which lasted almost 30 months and witnessed a decline of 83% in the NASDAQ Composite. This was the end of the great "dot.com" boom, which saw the Shiller CAPE attain an all-time high of 44, more than two-and-a-half times its long-term average. We can't confidently assign a SAFEMAX to this retiree, as his CAPE is literally "off the

Figure 13.1 CWR for 1 July 2000 and 31 October 1968 retirees (at 4.7% IWR). Standard configuration, seven asset classes.

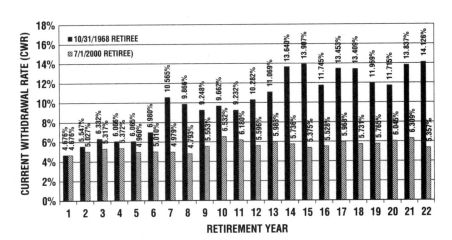

charts." This retiree also experienced a larger bear market in 2007–2009, the "COVID dip" in 2020, and a 25% decline in the S&P 500 in 2022. Rough seas in retirement, indeed!

Since we're testing for the failure of the Universal SAFEMAX, let's assume that this retiree had adopted the worst-case 4.7% initial withdrawal rate for their retirement. Figure 13.1 compares their CWR progress against the worst-case 1 October 1968 retiree for the first 22 years of retirement. This is the maximum period for which the 1 July 2000 retiree has actual, not extrapolated, data (as of this writing).

It's clear from the chart that even in the early years of retirement, the 1 July 2000 retiree had consistently much lower CWRs than the 1 October 1968 retiree. Nine full percentage points separate the two retirees in year #22, which is enormous. Suppose we assume that all investments earned average historical rates of return for years 23 through 30. In that case, the SAFEMAX for the 1 July 2000 retiree will be 5.53%, far above the 4.7% of the Universal SAFEMAX. Looking at it another way, the 1 July 2000 portfolio will last far longer than 30 years at the 4.7% IWR.

Over the next five years, it would take a market catastrophe of immense proportions to "break" the 4.7% rule, as far as the 1 July 2000 retiree is concerned. Instead, their problem may be having accumulated too much wealth at the end of retirement.

By the way, both retirees encountered multiple serious bear markets early in their retirement. What explains the difference in their SAFEMAX performance? It's simple: the 1968 investor experienced 6.1% annual inflation over the first 22 years, while the 2000 investor had only to contend with 2.9%. It wasn't bear markets but the inflation of their withdrawals that made the difference. Again, inflation presents itself as the worst enemy of retirees.

Let's look at one more contender for the "Bust the 4.7% rule" crown: the 1 October 2007 retiree. They retired into the worst stock bear market since the Great Depression; the S&P 500 lost 58% over only 18 months. In addition, they encountered the same COVID dip and 2022 slump as did the 1 January 2000 retiree, but almost seven years earlier in retirement. Figure 13.2 compares their CWR performance with that of the 10/1/1968 retiree.

Figure 13.2   Current withdrawal rate for 1 October 2007 and 31 October 1968 retirees (at 4.7% IWR). Standard configuration, seven asset classes.

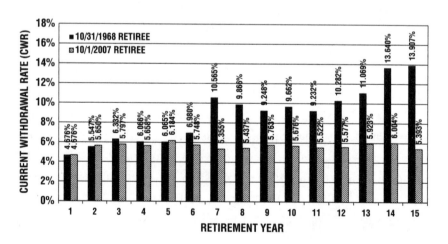

I have only 15 years of actual data for the 1 October 2007 retiree, so I restricted this chart to that interval. We don't want to get too froggy with our data! Once again, though, our suspect retiree has the superior CWR performance. In fact, looking at the 15-year milestone, the 2007 retiree performed marginally better than the 2000 retiree. Note that the 1968 retiree experienced 7.3% inflation over its first 15 years vs. 2.4% for the 2007 retiree.

There are preliminary indications that over the full 30 years, the 1 October 2007 retiree will not fare quite as well as the 1 January 2000 retiree. The former sports only a 5.22% SAFEMAX, albeit including 15 years of "averaged" data. But, once again, it does not appear the 1 October 2007 retiree is doomed to fail at the 4.7% SAFEMAX. It's probably too far ahead in the CWR race with the 1 October 1968 portfolio for this to occur, barring a sudden massive outbreak of inflation or 1929-style stock market collapse.

The only other likely recent candidate I can consider for failure is the 1 January 2022 retiree, who began retirement with a modest bear market and a brief inflation surge. Since then, the stock market has recovered, and inflation has declined considerably. However, it is far too early to draw any conclusions about the fate of the 1 January 2022 retiree. Please get back to me in about 15 years. If I'm no longer around, just chant "Beetlejuice" three times!

In summary, try as I can, I've been unable to identify a single retiree candidate for likely failure of the "4.7% rule." It's not that such an event can't or won't happen in the future; if it does, it'll probably result from the stubborn persistence of a high level of inflation. Even that would unlikely drop SAFEMAX down as low as 3%, as some have suggested. Those circumstances are difficult to imagine. For now, the "4.7% rule" still lives.

13.2 REQUIRED MINIMUM IRA DISTRIBUTIONS AND SAFEMAX

As you're probably aware, if you own a traditional IRA account that has escaped income taxation for many years, the tax code requires that after age 72 (soon to be 73), you must begin making annual distributions for the rest of your life (and pay income taxes on the amount withdrawn). These distributions begin at approximately 4% of the value of the IRA account, which percentage increases gradually over time. I have often entertained questions about whether following this "Required Minimum Distribution (RMD)" schedule adequately replaces a withdrawal plan.

I suspect this idea arose because of the closeness of the first-year RMD percentage (3.6%) to the original "4% rule." Let's study this issue using the "average SAFEMAX" 1 July 1989 retiree. We assume this individual retired at age 65 and planned for a 30-year planning horizon, using a tax-deferred account with all our "standard configuration." Figure 13.3 compares the CWR for the 1 July 1989 retiree using a SAFEMAX of 7.1% with the CWR under an RMD-only program. I displayed only the first 27 years of retirement to avoid distortions brought about by the very high CWR for the SAFEMAX plan in later years.

Pretty clearly, we're looking at two different animals! First, the SAFEMAX withdrawals begin at age 65, while the RMD withdrawals don't begin until age 72. If you follow the RMD program, that leaves seven years at the beginning of retirement with no income at all!

Furthermore, the SAFEMAX plan begins withdrawals at a much higher percentage of the portfolio than the RMD program, and this difference increases dramatically over time. Thus, the SAFEMAX plan generates far more retirement income than the RMD program. In year #27, for example, the SAFEMAX plan provides three times the withdrawals of the RMD program!

Figure 13.3   Current withdrawal rates for 1 July 1989 retiree (using 7.1% SAFEMAX vs. RMD withdrawals). Standard configuration, seven asset classes.

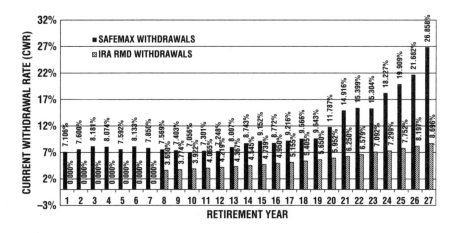

I hope this conclusively demonstrates that the RMD program is no substitute for a formal withdrawal plan and will make you feel like a pauper in retirement. Even if conditions are unfavorable and you feel compelled to withdraw at the Universal SAFEMAX (4.7%), the SAFEMAX plan is vastly superior (see Figure 13.4).

Figure 13.4 is constructed for a 50-year planning horizon, so that the SAFEMAX is as close as possible to the initial withdrawal rate under the RMD program. Because the planning horizon is 50 years instead of our standard 30, the Universal SAFEMAX is no longer 4.7%; it's about 4.2%. As you may recall, we previously discussed the effect of changing the planning horizon on SAFEMAX.

The same pattern emerges in the previous example for the first 25 years of retirement: CWR for the SAFEMAX plan is consistently higher than for the RMD program. However, the higher CWR belongs to the RMD program for years 26 through 47. In years 48 through 50 (which aren't shown to prevent distortions in scale), the higher CWR reverts to the SAFEMAX plan.

Figure 13.4   50-year current withdrawal rate for 1 July 1989 retiree (using 4.7% IWR vs. RMD withdrawals). Traditional IRA account, 50-year planning horizon, seven asset classes, fixed 55%/40%/5% stocks/bonds/cash.

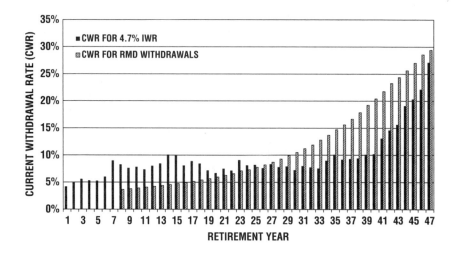

This phenomenon highlights a potential problem area in my research. Tax law requires one to withdraw at least the RMD amount, so the portfolio may be exhausted prematurely if that exceeds what is specified in the SAFEMAX plan. However, this applies only to plans for traditional IRA accounts with very long planning horizons and low initial withdrawal rates. I expect that most plans will be unaffected. However, you should be aware of this potential dilemma.

In sum, I don't believe that the RMD program represents a viable withdrawal plan for the vast majority of retirees. It usually causes one to enjoy far less income than under a conventional withdrawal plan.

If there is an advantage to the RMD program, it assures that your IRA portfolio will never run out of money. That's because beginning at age 120 and after that, annual withdrawals are frozen at 50% of the remaining account value. Time to party, old-timer!

13.3 SHOULD I "BUY-AND-HOLD"?

Virtually all my research assumes you will adopt a passive "buy-and-hold" strategy with your investments; that is to say, once bought, investments won't be sold except during account rebalancing or to fund withdrawals. There are several reasons I adopted this approach. First, it's almost impractical to analyze retirement portfolios not using this assumption. There are an infinite number of ways to invest other than buy-and-hold. Unless an alternative strategy has a mathematical formulation I can build into my spreadsheet models, evaluating its effect on withdrawal rates would be very difficult.

Second, most professional investment managers, particularly among financial planning firms, use the "buy-and-hold" approach. They have been schooled to do so, and it is a method that carries a minimum of "career risk." The latter phrase refers to the possibility of underperforming "the market," which can lead to client disappointment and eventual client defections. Furthermore, since most "active" fund managers have failed for many years to "beat the market," it seems sensible to employ a passive strategy that virtually assures clients they will do no worse than "market" returns.

However, using the "buy-and-hold" strategy in my analysis should not be construed as an endorsement of it. In fact, I strongly believe that retirees should use "risk management" techniques to protect their investments from the devastating effects of a major bear market.

What is "risk management"? I want to make it clear that it is not the same as "market timing," which consists of an attempt to outperform by selling all investments near a "top" in market prices and buying them all back at a "bottom" in prices. Markets are extremely difficult to predict, and identifying tops and bottoms (except in hindsight) can be virtually impossible. There are very few successful market timers, particularly over long time frames.

On the other hand, risk management means making gradual, incremental changes to your portfolio allocation (primarily in equities, but the concept can be extended to fixed-income investments as well) in response to one's assessment of market risk. "Risk" in this context means the probability of a significant decline in prices in the near future.

I've seen plenty of evidence to conclude this approach can be successful for retirees. Some have successfully used "moving average" techniques, whereby if 50-day average stock prices drop below their 200-day average, it triggers a signal to reduce stock exposure temporarily. Some use "momentum" metrics; others rely on technical analysis. There are many variations of this approach.

The question is, should you attempt this yourself? Some third-party subscription services provide guidance on what and when to buy and sell. One such service I use myself is InvesTech Research, based in Whitefish, Montana. They have had an excellent record in risk reduction for many years. There are others as well. If you don't manage your own money, you can locate money managers who take risk management seriously. I encourage you to investigate for yourself and find a service with which you are comfortable.

In any event, I believe it's important to use a third party in these matters, as investing can stir deep emotions (notably fear and greed), and neither of those emotions is conducive to a successful investment strategy. Remember, your goal in using risk management is not to "beat the market." It is to reduce the potential devastation a large bear market can have on your portfolio. Portfolios can, in a declining market, reach a "tipping point" from which they may be unable to recover their ability to generate the required sustainable income.

Protect your nest egg. Live to spend another day.

13.4 ANNUITIES

As an alternative to generating income from a portfolio of stocks and bonds, some retirees have turned to annuities. An annuity is a contractual agreement between an individual and a third party – usually an insurance company – for the third party to provide a continuing stream of income to the individual in exchange for a lump-sum payment by the individual, traditionally referred to as the "premium." The income stream is guaranteed for the individual's life, so the risk of exhausting one's income is thereby eliminated.

Annuities offer some unique advantages to retirees. For one, they remove investment risk from the shoulders of the individual and transfer it to the insurance company. No more worrying about the stock market and its volatility!

Furthermore, because they represent a large reservoir of funds collected from many individuals, the insurance company can offer higher payouts than if their capital was raised from just a few individuals. That's because some of the individual annuitants will die earlier than others, and their forfeited premiums are used to increase the benefits paid to survivors. This effect is called "longevity risk pooling." If you live well beyond your life expectancy, your cumulative annuity benefits could substantially exceed the benefits you might derive from self-investing your annuity premium. This is very much the same way other forms of insurance work.

Evidence has also been presented in the literature that retirees with annuities tend to spend more than those depending solely on income from their investment portfolio. This is related to the individual's sense that the annuity income stream is guaranteed, while investments can fluctuate in value and, in a worst-case scenario, become exhausted.

There are downsides to annuities as well, as with any financial product. The premium you pay for the annuity will reduce whatever legacy you plan to leave to your heirs. This could be particularly painful if you die shortly after annuity payments begin. There is also the risk that the insurance company's ability to pay becomes impaired, and you don't receive all the payments you contracted for. But that risk is very minimal if you select a financially sound insurance firm. And many states offer programs to protect annuitants against just such a disaster.

Annuities are available in simple forms and more complex varieties, which offer protection against inflation, stock market risk, and early death. Some of the more complicated forms can be difficult to understand, even for those who offer them. This can lead to unexpected and unpleasant outcomes for the buyer who does not perform their due diligence.

I'm not going to devote much more space in this book to the subject of annuities. That's not because I don't think they can be a useful tool for retirees, because I believe they can be. They represent a viable solution for some retirees concerned about outliving their income. It's just that I don't consider them financial investments, such as stocks and bonds, which are the primary focus of this book. I consider annuities an external source of income, such as Social Security or a pension plan, neither of which I discuss in this volume.

As my final word on this topic, I direct your attention to a 2001 study by Robert Veres, John Ameriks, and Mark Warshawsky, titled "Making Retirement Income Last a Lifetime" (see Appendix B). It was one of the first attempts to study the impact of buying an annuity on generating a higher sustainable retirement income.

Quoting from the paper: "Our analysis shows that the 4.5 percent withdrawal factor can be sustained with more certainty, for longer time periods, by adding the risk-pooling characteristics of an immediate annuity to the overall retirement portfolio. In much the same way as asset classes are used to hedge financial risks, immediate annuities can be used to hedge longevity risk."

13.5   WHEN THE SHILLER CAPE IS "OFF THE CHARTS"

Among the key components of my methodology are the "SAFEMAX finder" tables, which, for a given inflation regime, allow one to look up a value of SAFEMAX for a given value of the Shiller CAPE. However, those tables are based on historical data, and until fairly recently (July 1997), the CAPE had never exceeded its peak value of 32.6, attained in September of 1929. Since then, the Shiller CAPE has frequently exceeded that level, reaching a record of 44.2 in December 1999, at the height of the dot .com bubble.

Since 1997 was less than 30 years ago, we can't be sure of the values of SAFEMAX associated with such high values of Shiller CAPE, as no retiree has completed 30 years of retirement beginning at those levels. As a result, I am reluctant to include Shiller CAPE values much above the middle 20s in my tables. That poses a dilemma: What value of SAFEMAX should be used when Shiller CAPE is literally "off the charts"?

The Shiller CAPE is above 38 as I write these words, so this is a timely query. Regrettably, I can't frame a precise answer to the question now. We won't know for years, even decades, the correct SAFEMAX for many of the high-CAPE retirees.

However, we can draw some tentative conclusions based on the examination of results for those who retired from 1 April 1993 to 1 April 2013. For this purpose, let's return to Figure 4.1 and study the COLA scheme curve. It contains SAFEMAX values for retirees through 1 January 2013. As noted earlier, none of the retirees from 1 April 1993 to 1 April 2013 has a full 30 years of data in their matrixes. Some have as few as 10 years.

Nonetheless, earlier, we concluded that the fate of a retirement portfolio is frequently determined in its first 10–12 years. Thus, it's reasonable to expect that there will not be significant future changes to any of the SAFEMAX values for these portfolios, even if they contain extrapolated data.

Given that assumption, we note that between 1 July 1997 and 1 July 2001, there were 17 retirees with Shiller CAPE between 32 and 44. According to Figure 4.1, none of these retirees had a SAFEMAX less than about 5.4%. This is a very encouraging result. It suggests that the Shiller CAPE/SAFEMAX curves (as in Figures 2.8, 2.9, and 2.10) all "shallow out" at high values of Shiller CAPE. That means that very high CAPE values do not necessarily produce very low SAFEMAX values.

This conclusion might change in coming years, but my answer to the question "What SAFEMAX should I use for off-the-chart Shiller CAPEs?" is "just a bit less than the highest SAFEMAX currently on the chart." Typically, a SAFEMAX between 5.25% and 5.5% appears approximately correct. I see no need to go as low as the "Universal SAFEMAX" of 4.7% unless inflation again becomes a serious problem.

13.6   IS IT SCIENCE?

My fellow retirement researcher, Abraham Okusanya, is passionately devoted to a scientific approach, as evidenced by the title of his book *Beyond the 4% Rule: The Science of Retirement Portfolios That Last a Lifetime* (see Appendix A). As is my friend, I'm an advocate for a scientific approach. But what do we exactly mean by that phrase? And can what I have presented in this book be considered "science"? Let's talk about that a bit.

All science involves the application of "the scientific method": careful observation of phenomena (natural and otherwise) and an attempt to accurately describe, explain, and predict their behavior. This certainly applies to economics, of which "retirement planning" is a subset. We have many fine researchers today studying retirement income issues and writing multitudinous articles and books on the subject: Wade Pfau, Michael Kitces, David Blanchett, Jonathan Guyton, Larry Swedroe, Moshe Milevsky, William Klinger, Abraham Okusanya, Michael Finke, Christine Benz, Laurence Kotlikoff, Scott Burns, Jim C. Otar, Robert Veres, John Ameriks, Mark Warshawsky, William F. Sharpe, William Richenstein, Harold Evensky, Michael McClung, Tom Canfield, Ryan McLean, Michael K. Stein, Zvi Bodie, Gordon Pye, Karsten Jeske, and so on (I apologize to anyone whose name I have omitted).

However, if you were expecting a presentation of grand Laws and Theories of retirement income (equivalent to Newton's Laws of Motion and Einstein's Theory of Relativity) in this book, you would have been sorely disappointed. And if you were expecting cogent mathematical expressions that could predict essential aspects of retirement income, such as "$E = mc^2$," you have similarly found the cupboard empty. They just don't exist in my field (sorry, the "4.7% rule" doesn't count!). The most advanced math I've used in this book is algebra, which many of you learned in high school. Currently, I see no justification for much more than that.

This is because economics is a social science that deals with manifestations of human behavior. As you can probably guess, human behavior is a lot tougher to analyze and predict than the energy released by a nuclear explosion or the effects of the sun's gravity on the orbit of Jupiter, which are in the province of physics, a natural science. Natural sciences have the advantage that their phenomena are representable by laws, theories, and mathematical precision. Physicists can actually *predict* matters relating to their science. It's a facility that we don't enjoy.

The best we have been able to do so far is to study retirement behavior, describe what's happened in the past, and build mathematical constructs to replicate that behavior. We have no underlying theories and associated mathematics we can use to predict what will happen in the future. Ours is an empirical science relying on observation, categorization, and model-building. Any prediction we might make about future behavior is merely an extrapolation of past behavior and could be invalidated by a change in that behavior.

What sorts of things in the economic sphere could be different than they have been in the past, and how could they impact retirement income planning? Here are a few examples:

1. Some observers have postulated that in the US, slower future population growth could lead to lower profit growth for US corporations, and consequently lower returns for US stocks. If this were to occur, future withdrawal rates could be reduced significantly.

2. As a counterpoint to #1, the evolution of Artificial Intelligence could dramatically improve human productivity, boosting the growth of GDP and corporate profits. This could have a positive effect on withdrawal rates if these effects are reflected in stock prices.

3. Business regulations could change, perhaps in response to climate change, social upheaval, etc. Some already claim we should not be using stock market data prior to the major market regulations of the 1930s and 1940s, as these fundamentally changed the ways in which markets operated. Similar changes could occur in the future.

4. After a substantial period of low inflation and declining interest rates, we may be headed into a lengthy regime of higher inflation and higher interest rates, for various reasons (de-globalization, excessive government debt, continued deficit spending). We have already discussed the ominous threat higher inflation represents to withdrawal rates.

5. Large-scale wars could damage business assets and reduce business profits, causing chaos in stock markets around the globe. This could reduce the dependability of returns from financial assets we have all come to expect, which underlies the past level of withdrawal rates.

As usual, there is always something to worry about, and often the worst never comes to pass! Nevertheless, the above list underscores the difficulty of making predictions in our field. I shrink from using the word "predictions" as applied to any aspect of my work. When I present information about withdrawal rates, I consider myself more as a reporter of what has occurred in the past than as a Nostradamus prophesying what will occur in the future. I urge you to adopt a healthy skepticism toward anyone who claims differently.

Returning to my original question, can what I and my fellow researchers do in this field be called science? I reply "Yes!" because we follow scientific methods and principles. We have made great strides in understanding our phenomena, through the development of fields such as "behavioral finance," which studies how human biases cause us to make bad financial decisions.

The fact that we lack advanced theories and predictive tools should not be held against us because this also applies to other sciences. And who knows? Perhaps someday, some genius such as Hari Seldon in Isaac Asimov's "Foundation" novels will provide us with the theoretical and mathematical basis to do what physicists can do with atoms, planets, and galaxies today: accurately portray their interactions and futures.

Till then, please read and use our work, but recognize its limitations. As the great Warren Buffett has opined, it is more important to be approximately correct than precisely wrong.

13.7 SHOULD I WAIT FOR A HIGHER SAFEMAX TO RETIRE?

Figure 2.6 shows that 30-year SAFEMAX has varied widely over time, from a worst-case low of less than 5% to a Himalayan-like peak of over 16%. What's also apparent from the figure is that dramatic changes in SAFEMAX have occurred in relatively short periods. For example, the 1 October 1931 retiree (retiree A) registered a SAFEMAX of about 9.6%. Just nine months later, the 1 July 1932 retiree (retiree B) enjoyed a 16.2% SAFEMAX, or almost double that of the earlier retiree. How can there be such a huge divergence in SAFEMAX between two retirement dates so close together? And how does it impact the decision on when to retire?

We should note that the two retirees, having retired only nine months apart, share data for 117 out of 120 quarters. That seems to make it even less probable they would have such a significant disparity between their SAFEMAX. The key to understanding the difference is to recognize that retiree A suffered a −23% loss in their portfolio in the first nine months of retirement, while retiree B (retiring just after the Depression Bear Market bottom) enjoyed a gain of almost +25% in their first nine months. That's quite a reversal of fortune.

This 50% spread in investment returns, occurring early in retirement, accounts for much of the dramatic difference in their withdrawal rates. This observation begs the next question: Should the October 1931 retiree curse their luck and dearly regret not retiring nine months later?

Let's take a closer look at how these two retirees fared. Figure 13.5 tracks the annual dollar withdrawals for each of the two retirees during the first 10 years after retirement. Each retiree has a balance of $100,000 in their tax-advantaged account on 1 October 1931 (yes, I know, IRAs didn't exist then).

Figure 13.5   Annual withdrawals for retiree A (1 October 1931) vs. retiree B (1 July 1932). Standard configuration, seven asset classes, first 10 years, retiree A start $100,000, retiree B start $77,526.

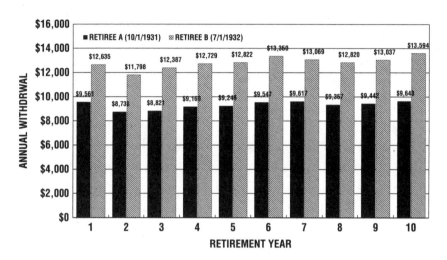

Each is also assumed to withdraw using their individual SAFEMAX: for retiree A, this is 9.6%, and for retiree B, 16.2%. However, the portfolio value of retiree A at their retirement date is $100,000, while that of retiree B begins retirement at $77,500 due to losses in stocks in the prior nine months. As you can see in Figure 13.5, retiree B does come out on top each year by a substantial margin. Over the first 10 years of retirement, retiree B's withdrawals average about 38% above those of their counterpart. However, this is far less than we initially feared from the 70% difference in their SAFEMAX. Nonetheless, in this case, it would have been better financially if retiree A had waited nine months to retire.

It should be pointed out that this is an extreme example, the largest disparity between two SAFEMAX rates for nearby retirees in the historical record. Furthermore, while the portfolio fell −23% in the nine months between October 1931 and July 1932, ***the Shiller CAPE fell by almost one-half.*** This established one of the cheapest US stock markets ever, creating a "coiled spring" for retiree B's portfolio to rebound spectacularly and generate an extraordinarily high SAFEMAX.

Most historical disparities in SAFEMAX for adjoining retirement dates are far smaller than the preceding one. One example is retiree C (retiring 1 October 1989 with a SAFEMAX of 7.06%) and retiree D (retiring 1 October 1990 with a SAFEMAX of 8.80%). That's almost a 25% increase in SAFEMAX in just one year. How will that translate into a difference in withdrawals, though?

Figure 13.6 compares the two retirees' first 10 years of dollar withdrawals. Retiree D, the later retiree, again has higher withdrawals, but this time by a far more modest margin. Retiree D's withdrawals average only about 10% more than those of retiree C. Note that owing to a modest stock bear market in 1990, retiree D begins retirement with a portfolio of approximately $90,600, less than the $100,000 of retiree C. This mitigates the large spread in SAFEMAX between the two retirees.

Figure 13.6   Annual withdrawals for retiree C (1 October 1989) vs. retiree D (1 July 1990). Standard configuration, seven asset classes, first 10 years, retiree C start $100,000, retiree D start $85,327.

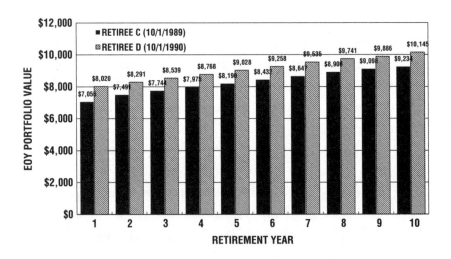

The lesson we have learned from this analysis is that delaying retirement in hopes of lower stock prices can be beneficial in terms of higher withdrawals. However, the improvement may often be modest and could be outweighed by personal considerations. Furthermore, given the unpredictability of markets, the wait for a better financial opportunity to retire may be far longer than anticipated.

CHAPTER 14

GO FORTH AND PLAN!

It's time for you to roll up your sleeves and create your own personal retirement withdrawal plan. In this book, I've provided you with most of the necessary tools. I wish I could sit at your elbow and guide you through the process, but book technology has not yet progressed to that point. Perhaps AI will someday get us there.

One thing I can do is offer to answer any general questions you have through my website. I'm no longer a practicing financial advisor, so it wouldn't be appropriate for me to answer questions specific to your own situation, such as "Should I withdraw first from my Roth IRA or my taxable account?" or "Do you think I should plan to withdraw more money to cover medical expenses?" Those questions are best posed to an active financial advisor.

However, I'd be happy to answer general questions about my research, such as "Which SAFEMAX finder table seems best for this environment?"

or "Please explain the SAFEMAX concept to me." Just visit my website, select "Ask Bill," and type in your question. I'll answer it as soon as I can. Please be patient; I get a lot of inquiries!

In addition to answering questions, I'm building a library of charts on my website for you to download to assist in developing your plan. This book contains many charts, but it would require hundreds, if not thousands, to represent the many combinations of factors in my research. That is far beyond the scope of the present work.

For example, I plan to develop "SAFEMAX finder tables" not only for the COLA withdrawal scheme (tables for which appear in this book) but for all the other withdrawal schemes I study, including "Front-Loaded" and "Fixed Percentage" withdrawal schemes. This library will take some time to establish, but the good news is there will be no "late charges"!

Before we part, let's summarize the key points I have made in this book:

1. The "4.7% rule" is a rule only if you accept ten underlying assumptions (i.e., the standard configuration of the eight Elements, high inflation, and high market valuation).

2. Planning for your withdrawals is a formal, organized activity. Don't take any shortcuts, or you may end up in an uncomfortable place. Select options for each of the eight Elements, ascertain your Shiller CAPE, decide on an inflation regime, and create an appropriate template chart.

3. Give yourself margins for error in your planning, wherever possible. For example, be generous with your planning horizon. Plan to see your grandchildren's children! It's much easier to increase your withdrawals than it is to reduce them.

4. Retirement withdrawal planning is not a formal science such as physics. It is an empirical science. We rely on history to guide us. We have no theories or formulas with which to accurately predict the future. Thus, we extrapolate past results into the future at our own risk.

5. SAFEMAX is a valuable concept, representing the highest withdrawal rate attainable by an individual historical retiree without exhausting their portfolio prematurely. The SAFE component of the term is "safe" only in historical context. One can't guarantee the safety of any withdrawal plan in the future. Indeed, I can't provide such a guarantee!

6. Universal SAFEMAX represents the worst-case individual SAFEMAX for all retirees for a given set of values of the eight Elements. This concept is the basis for the "4.7% rule." Universal SAFEMAX has declined in the past and may well decline again in the future. Note that it applies to less than 1% of all historical retirees; all the others enjoyed a higher individual SAFEMAX, some much higher.

7. I have identified ten variables in withdrawal planning. Eight of them, which I call "Elements," involve matters of personal choice. The other two, inflation and stock market valuation, reflect market conditions. They offer little if any choice to the retiree. All ten are equally crucial to the final plan, although, as in the book *Animal Farm*, some are admittedly more equal than others.

8. Because it is usually long-term, a withdrawal plan needs to be managed. It can't be left to fend for itself for thirty or forty years. It must be monitored, assessed for problems, and "fixed" if needed.

9. My research is based on buying and holding all investments, selling only during portfolio rebalancing. But a retiree may choose another approach, including risk management. If so, consider using a third party to guide your efforts. Investing is challenging enough without getting our emotions involved.

10. If stocks are relatively expensive, and you can do so, it may be financially beneficial to defer retirement until after the next stock

bear market. You may enjoy a considerably higher SAFEMAX, which will mean a more prosperous lifestyle in retirement. However, the length of the wait is uncertain, and other considerations may be of greater priority.

11. A withdrawal plan is not forever. It can be modified or terminated at any time during retirement. A new plan may be started at any time with a completely new set of assumptions.

12. When investing for retirement, remember the four "free lunches": diversification, timely rebalancing, tilting your equity allocation slightly toward small-company and micro-cap stocks, and rising glidepath investing. These all add to your withdrawal rate without incurring any additional risk.

13. Inflation is the greatest enemy of retirees. Make early and decisive adjustments to your withdrawal plan if sustained high inflation becomes a serious threat.

Best of luck with your withdrawal plan! Don't hesitate to get help from a qualified professional if needed. And most of all, enjoy your retirement! Isn't that why you saved all that money over all those years?

APPENDIX A

BOOKS WORTH READING

Benz, Christine. *How to Retire: 20 Lesson for a Happy, Successful and Wealthy Retirement*. Hardcover. Harriman House, 2024.

Bernstein, William. *The Intelligent Asset Allocator: How to Build Your Portfolio to Maximize Returns and Minimize Risk*. Paperback. McGraw-Hill Education, 2017.

Canfield, Tom. *Nest Egg Care*. Paperback workbook. Self-published, 2017.

Cygan, Donna Skeels. *The Joy of Financial Security*. Hardcover. Sage Future Press, 2013.

Evensky, Harold and Deena B. Katz. *Retirement Income Redesigned: Master Plans for Distribution*. Bloomberg Press, 2006.

Gotto, Bradly J. *Spending Money and Having Fun*. Paperback. Lioncrest Publishing, 2022.

Jalinski, Josh. *Retirement Reality Check: How to Spend Your Money and Still Leave an Amazing Legacy*. Paperback. HarperCollins Leadership, 2019.

Kotlikoff, Laurence J. and Scott Burns. *Spend 'til the End*. Hardcover. Simon & Schuster, 2008.

Krantz, Matt. *Retirement Planning for Dummies*. Paperback. Wiley, 2020.

McClung, Michael H. *Living Off Your Money: The Modern Mechanics of Investing During Retirement With Stocks and Bonds*. Paperback. Self-published, 2015.

Milevsky, Moshe A. *The 7 Most Important Equations for Your Retirement*. Hardcover. Wiley, 2012.

Netti, Frank L. *Retire Sooner Retire Richer*. Paperback. McGraw-Hill, 2003.

Okusanya, Abraham. *Beyond the 4% Rule*. Paperback. 2017.

Otar, Jim C. *High Expectations & False Dreams*. Paperback. Self-published, 2001.

Pfau, Wade. *How Much Can I Spend in Retirement*. Paperback. Self-published, 2018.

Quinn, Jane Bryant. *How to Make Your Money Last: The Indispensable Retirement Guide*. Hardcover. Simon & Schuster, 2016.

Savage, Terry. *The New Savage Number: How Much Money Do You REALLY Need to Retire?* Paperback. Wiley, 2009.

Stein, Michael K. *The Prosperous Retirement: Guide to the New Reality*. Paperback. EMSTCO Press, 1998.

Swedroe, Larry and Kevin Grogan. *Reducing the Risk of Black Swans: Using the Science of Investing to Capture Returns with Less Volatility*. Paperback. BAM Alliance Press, 2018.

Swedroe, Larry and Kevin Grogan. *Your Complete Guide to a Successful & Secure Retirement*. Paperback. Harriman House, 2019.

APPENDIX B

ARTICLES WORTH READING

PORTFOLIO WITHDRAWAL STRATEGIES

Blanchett, David. "Guided Spending Rates: Rethinking 'Safe' Initial Withdrawal Rates," *PGIM DC Solutions*, April 2024.

Blanchett, David, Fink, Michael and Pfau, Wade D. "Low Bond Yields and Safe Portfolio Withdrawal Rates," *Morningstar Investment Management*, January 2013.

Guyton, Jonathan. "Decision Rules and Portfolio Management for Retirees: Is the Safe Initial Withdrawal Rate Too Safe?" The *Journal of Financial Planning*, March 2006.

Guyton, Jonathan and William Klinger. "Decision Rules and Maximum Initial Withdrawal Rates." *The Journal of Financial Planning*, October 2010.

Kitces, Michael. "Is the Safe Withdrawal Rate Sometimes Too Safe?" *The Kitces Report*, May 2008.

Kitces, Michael. "Investment Costs, Taxes, and the Safe Withdrawal Rate," *The Kitces Report*, February 2010.

Kitces, Michael. "Are Retirement Bucket Strategies an Asset Allocation Mirage?" *kitces.com*, April 2012.

Kitces, Michael. "Managing Sequence of Return Risk With Bucket Strategies Vs a Total Return Rebalancing Approach," *kitces.com*, November 2014.

Milevsky, Moshe and Huaxion Huang. "Retirement Spending on Planet Vulcan: Longevity Risk and Withdrawal Rates." *AAII Journal*, January 2018.

Pfau, Wade D. "Variable Withdrawals in Retirement." *Advisor Perspectives*, April 2012.

Pfau, Wade D. "Four Approaches to Managing Retirement Income Risk (Pfau)." *The American College for Financial Services*, November 2023.

TAXES AND SAFE WITHDRAWAL RATES

Kitces, Michael. "Investment Costs, Taxes, and the Safe Withdrawal Rate." *The Kitces Report*, February 2019.

ANNUITIES

Blanchett, David M. "Impact of Guaranteed Income and Dynamic Withdrawals on Safe Initial Withdrawal Rates," *Journal of Financial Planning*, April 2017.

Finke, Michael and Pfau, Wade D. "Reduce Retirement Costs with DIA Purchased Before Retirement," *Journal of Financial Planning*, July 2015.

Milevsky, Moshe. "Annuity Fables." *Journal of Financial Planning*, December 2018.

Veres, Robert et al. "Making Retirement Income Last a Lifetime," *Journal of Financial Planning*, December 2001.

Warshawsky, Mark. "New Approaches to Retirement Income: An Evaluation of Combination Laddered Strategies," *Journal of Financial Planning*, August 2016.

ASSET ALLOCATION

Blanchett, David M. and Finke, Michael. "Annuitized Income and Optimum Equity Allocation," *Journal of Financial Planning*, November 2018.

Blanchett, David M. and Finke, Michael. "The False Promise of U.S. Historical Returns," *Advisor Perspectives*, March 2021.

Blanchett, David M. and Stempien, Jeremy. "Investment Horizon, Serial Correlation, and Better (Retirement) Portfolios," *CFA Institute Research Foundation*, April 2024.

Blanchett, David M. and Stempien, Jeremy. "Commodities for the Long Run," *CFA Enterprising Investor*, July 2024.

Cooley, Philip L. et al. "Does International Diversification Increase the Sustainable Withdrawal Rates from Retirement Portfolios?" *Journal of Financial Planning*, January 2003.

Horneff, Walter J. et al. "Optimizing the Retirement Portfolio: Asset Allocation, Annuitization, and Risk Aversion," *National Bureau of Economic Research working paper 12392*, July 2006.

Huebscher, Robert. "The Simplest, Safest Withdrawal Strategy (TIPS)," *Advisor Perspectives*, August 2011.

Kitces, Michael. "Dynamic Asset Allocation and Safe Withdrawal Rates," *The Kitces Report*, April 2009.

McLean, Ryan. "How Diversification Improves Safe Withdrawal Rates," *Advisor Perspectives*, December 2020.

Nawrocki, David N. and Evensky, Harold. "Dynamic Asset Allocation During Different Inflation Scenarios," *Journal of Financial Planning*, October 2003.

Otar, Jim C. "The Secret Formula," *Financial Planning*, October 2003.

Richenstein, William. "How to Calculate an After-Tax Asset Allocation," *Journal of Financial Planning*, August 2008.

PORTFOLIO REBALANCING

Darnyani, Gobind. "Money for Nothing," *Inside Information*, November 2005.

Weiss, Gerald F. "Dynamic Rebalancing," *Journal of Financial Planning*, February 2001.

DECISION RULES AND GUARD-RAIL INVESTING

Kitces, Michael E. "Accelerating Rising Equity Glidepath Using Treasury Bills as Portfolio Ballast?" *Kitces.com*, August 2014.

Kitces, Michael E. "Valuation-Based Tactical Asset Allocation in Retirement and the Impact of Market Valuation on Declining and Rising Equity Glidepaths," *Kitces.com*, September 2014.

Kitces, Michael E. and Pfau, Wade D. "Retirement Risk, Rising Equity Glidepaths, and Valuation-Based Asset Allocation," *Journal of Financial Planning*, March 2015.

Klinger, William J. "Guardrails to Prevent Retirement Portfolio Failure," *Journal of Financial Planning*, October 2016.

Pfau, Wade D. and Kitces, Michael E. "Reducing Retirement Risk with a Rising Equity Glide Path," *Journal of Financial Planning*, January 2014.

WITHDRAWAL SCHEMES

Blanchett, David. "Exploring the Retirement Consumption Puzzle," *Journal of Financial Planning*, May 2014.

Sharpe, William F. et al. "Efficient Retirement Financial Strategies," *Pension Research Council*, March 2007.

PORTFOLIO REBALANCING

McLean, Ryan. "Rebalancing Frequency and Safe Withdrawal Rates," *Finding: Advisor Perspectives*, 12 April 2021.

Spitzer, John J. and Sandeep Singh. "Is Rebalancing a Portfolio During Retirement Necessary?" *Journal of Financial Planning*, June 2007.

Tomlinson, Joe. "Does Rebalancing Help Investors in the Withdrawal Phase?" *Advisor Perspectives*, 11 January 2021.

REQUIRED MINIMUM DISTRIBUTIONS AND WITHDRAWALS

Israelson, Craig. "How Skillful RMD Planning Can Sustain Retirement Portfolios," *Financial Planning magazine*, March 2017.

Spitzer, John J. "Do Required Minimum Distributions Endanger 'Safe' Portfolio Withdrawal Rates?" *Journal of Financial Planning*, August 2008.

Sun, Wei and Anthony Webb. "Should Households Base Asset Decumulation Strategies on Required Minimum Distribution Tables?" Center for Retirement Research at Boston College, April 2012.

APPENDIX C

SOFTWARE WORTH USING

"The Big Picture" application: bigpicapp.co. Founded by Ryan McLean. Determines "success rate of withdrawal rates by varying asset allocation and planning horizon."

ABOUT
THE AUTHOR

William P. Bengen received a B.S. from M.I.T. in Aeronautics and Astronautics and an M.S. from the College for Financial Planning. He has had four careers: trained as an aerospace engineer, CEO of his family's soft drink bottling business (NY), fee-only financial planning practitioner (CA), and currently a financial researcher and aspiring novelist (AZ). He is a former CFP® licensee. In the early 1990s, in response to client questions, Mr. Bengen began research on the sustainability of withdrawals from stock and bond portfolios, which gave rise to the so-called "4% Rule." He is frequently quoted in major financial publications, and appears regularly on financial industry podcasts. In 2014 he received NAPFA's **Robert J. Underwood Distinguished Service Award** and in 2017 the **InvestmentNews Innovators Award**. In 2023 he was awarded the **Inside Information Iconoclast Award**. He currently lives in SaddleBrooke, AZ, where he continues his research into the "4% Rule."

INDEX

Page numbers followed by *f* and *t* refer to figures and tables, respectively.